mini ARTISTS

mini ARTISTS

20 projects inspired by the great artists

Joséphine Seblon

illustrated by Robert Sae-Heng

Contents

mini
ARTISTS OF THE PAST

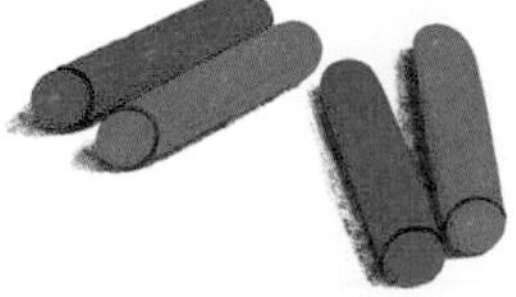

mini
MODERN ARTISTS

mini
CONTEMPORARY ARTISTS

INTRODUCTION

"Those who do not want to imitate anything, produce nothing."

SALVADOR DALÍ

Every artist's journey begins with looking at and imitating other artists. Visual artists, architects, and designers all draw inspiration from other artists, past and present, when creating their own work. Over time, these experiences allow them to explore art history and discover their own style and voice.

One day, I was wondering how I could get my two young children engaged with art when I had an idea. If artists are looking at the work of other artists for inspiration, what can mini artists learn from art history? I wanted my children's enthusiasm for making to translate into a love of the visual arts, old and new. And I could see that knowledge of art history would feed their imagination and stimulate their creativity. That's how this book was born.

Each of the twenty projects in this book provides an opportunity for your mini artist to learn about a famous artwork and think about what makes it special, and then to make their own mini masterpiece by following easy step-by-step instructions. From projects inspired by the Pech Merle cave to the dotty world of Yayoi Kusama, I've tried and tested every activity with my children. I've also made sure the materials are easy to get a hold of and the time for set-up and clean-up is minimal. That means you can focus on the good stuff–spending quality time together, having fun, and making mini masterpieces.

Joséphine Seblon

Pablo Picasso, *Claude Dessinant, Françoise et Paloma*, 1950

How to use this book

Build a craft box

Each project lists the materials you will need, but it can be helpful to have extra materials on hand for when you're feeling creative. Build a craft box with the essentials: white paper, colored paper, pencils, washable paints, playdough, scissors, and glue. You could add recycled materials such as cardboard, sponges, toothbrushes, paper straws, and tinfoil.

Pick the right project

Each project takes five minutes to set up and five minutes to clean up, but the fun lasts for as long as your mini artist remains engaged. So it's always worth choosing a project that suits their mood! Keep in mind your mini artist's interests, the techniques they might enjoy and the materials you have on hand.

Discover different techniques

There are many ways to bring subjects to life. Work with your mini artist to explore the most popular techniques, and remember to experiment. Why stop at drawing and painting? Try cutting, modeling, assembling, carving and sculpting, mosaic, printing, installation, and more.

Make it your own

Your mini artist will take inspiration from amazing artists from around the world, but there's no need to copy any of the projects exactly–the fun of art is exploring your own ideas. If they are obsessed with dinosaurs, make a dinosaur mosaic! Are they into space? A stained-glass solar system will go down well. The art world is your oyster!

mini
ARTISTS
OF THE
PAST

Have you ever wondered how art from the distant past is relevant today? Many famous artists were drawn to the "origins" of art. This means they were interested in the works of early artists–and many of today's mini artists feel the same way.

Looking at ancient art can be so inspiring. The artists of the past have experimented with lots of different techniques over the centuries–the best of which you will be able to try here. There will be drawing and painting, of course, but also spraying, printing, modeling, and projects inspired by stained glass and mosaic making. From the very beginning, artists were interested in creating images of the things they could see around them: animals, human hands and faces, and the landscape. Join them in picturing the beauty of the world as you see it.

Ice Age stencils

The Pech Merle horses

Look at this!

Horse paintings at Pech Merle cave, *c.* 15,000 BCE

This activity is inspired by cave paintings made thousands of years ago at the Pech Merle cave in France. The artists used pipes made of bone to blow pigment onto the cave walls. They used their hands as stencils.

Discuss this!

Imagine you are standing inside a cave house. The photo above shows how the walls were decorated. Can you believe that these artists were allowed to draw on the walls?

- What did these cave artists draw?
- Can you see two animals? What are they?
- Can you count their spots?
- Can you see hands and feet?

Give it a try!

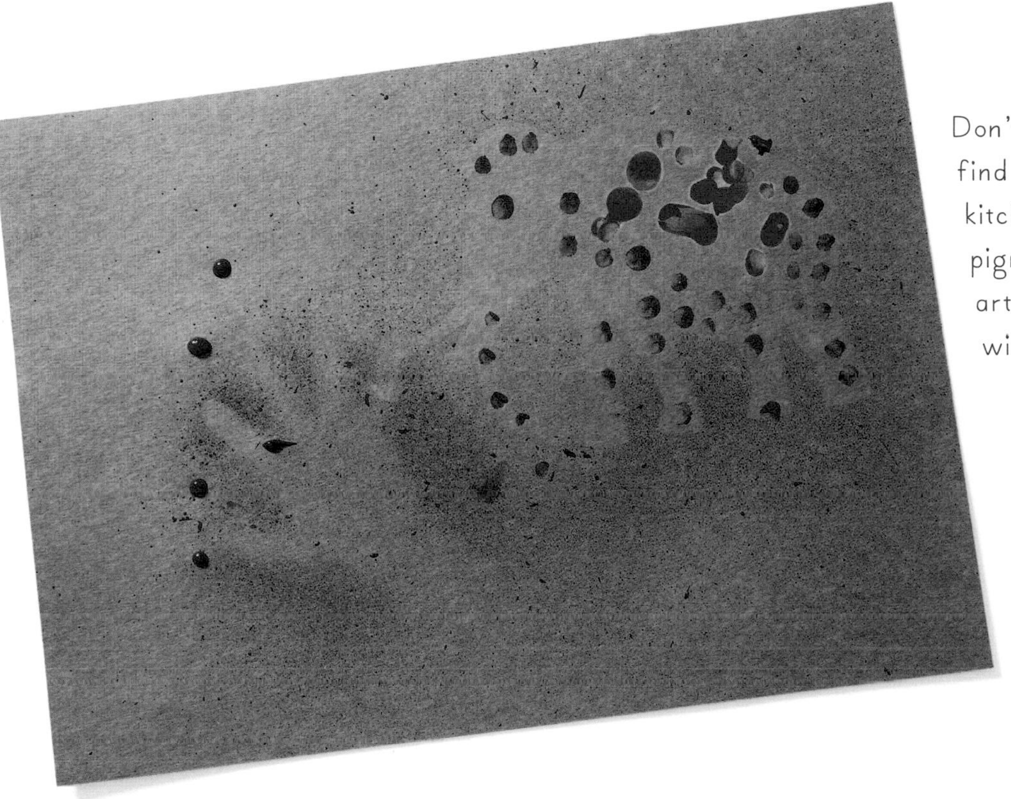

Don't worry if you can't find a bone pipe in the kitchen drawer to spray pigment like the ancient artists–a toothbrush will do the trick!

You will need:

- Washable paint in red and brown
- 2 small bowls
- A bowl or glass of water
- A toothbrush (old or unwanted)
- Paper (Kraft paper is ideal because it looks just like a cave wall!)
- Scissors

Remember to put down some newspaper first–cave art can get messy.

1

Add brown paint and red paint to two small bowls. Place one hand on a piece of paper.

2

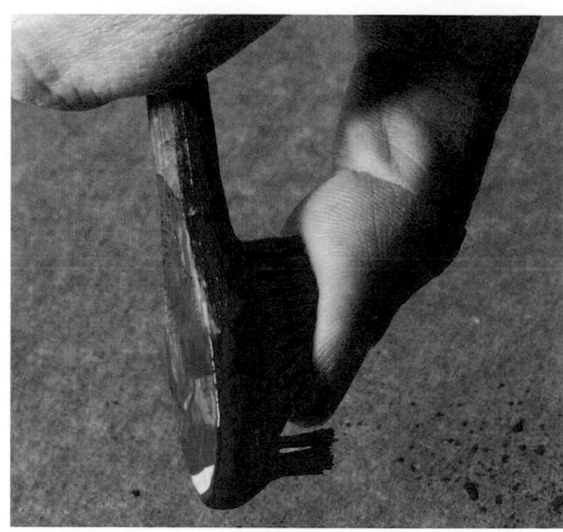

Dip the toothbrush in the red paint and flick it using your thumb to make it spray. Spray the paint around the edge of the hand that's on the paper.

3

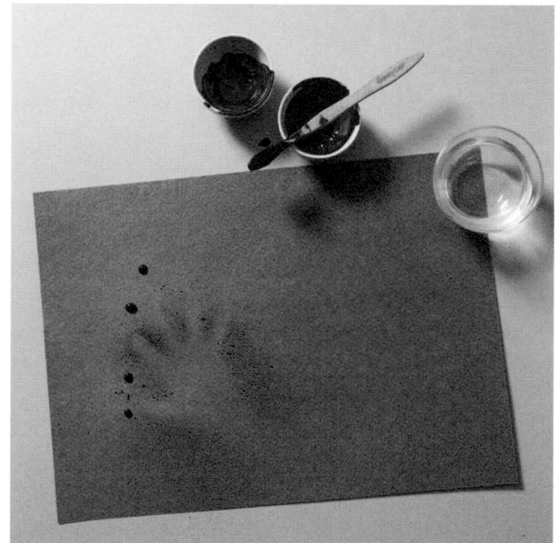

Keep flicking until there is paint sprayed all around your hand. Wait a few minutes while the paint dries, then remove your hand.

4

Next, cut the shape of an animal from another piece of paper. Place it next to the stenciled hand on the paper.

Tip! This technique requires careful motor control. If your mini artist finds this tricky, take turns flicking paint onto each other's hands.

5

Flick brown paint around the edges of the cut-out animal, using the same technique as before. Remove the animal shape when you're done.

6

Dip your fingertips in paint to add some extra decorative patterns, such as dots, on top of your animal and hand stencils.

Try this!

Stencils aren't the only way to capture the outline of an animal or shape. Why not try tracing shadows instead? Place a toy on a piece of paper on a sunny day, and draw around the outline of the shadow that the toy casts on the paper. Tracing is a great way to improve observation skills!

Symbols on clay

Sumerian cuneiform tablets

Look at this!

Sumerian tablet, *c.* 2350 BCE

Tablets like this were made by ancient Sumerians in Mesopotamia. They are examples of the earliest known form of writing, in a script called "cuneiform." The lines, shapes, and symbols in this tablet record the number of goats and sheep that were looked after by a Sumerian shepherd.

Discuss this!

Imagine how a letter or postcard might look to an alien. They'd probably think it was full of mysterious symbols, just like these tablets look to us!

- What do you think this tablet could be? Could it be a recipe, a calendar, or a treasure map?
- Can you recognize any shapes? Perhaps you can see triangles, or little moons?
- What do you think these symbols mean?

Give it a try!

Invent your own ancient script to write a secret message on a clay tablet.

You will need:

- Air-dry clay
- Child-friendly knife and fork (or straws, sticks, or clay-working tools, such as a stylus)

Clay can stick to surfaces, so remember to work on a tablecloth or outside if you prefer.

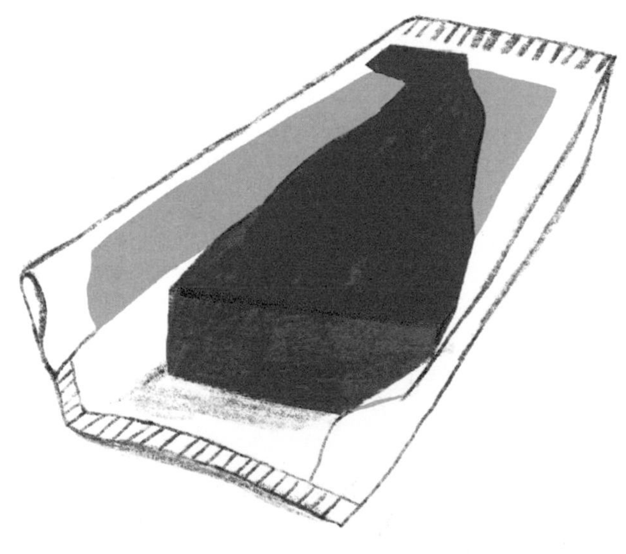

1

Mold a piece of clay into a nice ball.

2

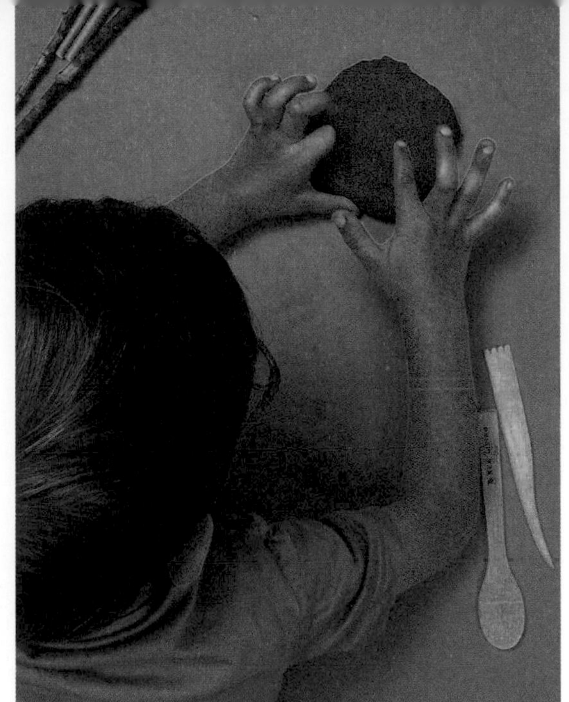

Use your hands to squash your clay ball down into a flat square. This will be your tablet.

3

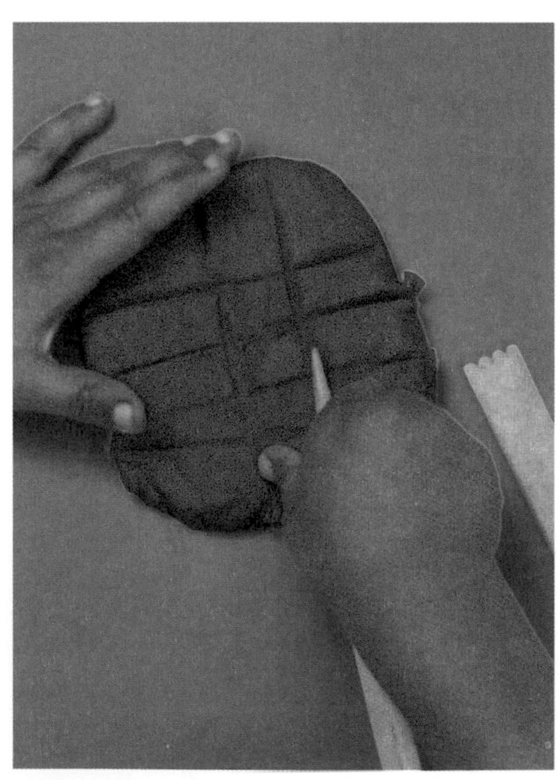

Drag your child-friendly knife or clay-working tools across the surface of the tablet. Draw horizontal and vertical lines to form a grid of little boxes.

4

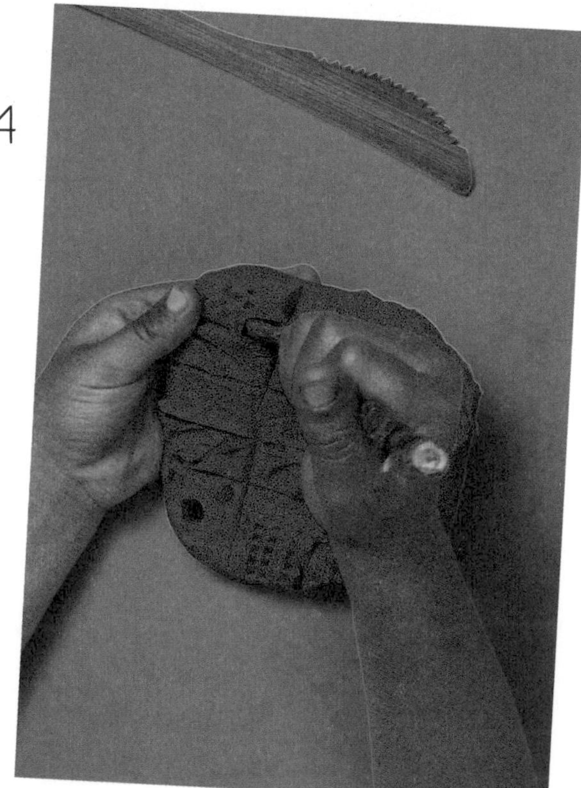

Time to write your secret message! Use your tools or a stick to draw cuneiform-like characters into each box. You could use all sorts of shapes, like dots, stars, squares, circles, and moons.

Let your cuneiform tablet dry. Your secret message is ready!

Tip! You can correct any mistakes by moistening the clay with water to erase the marks.

Try this!

Next time you work with clay, why not try a stamping technique? First, shape the clay into a long, thick strip (a rolling pin can help). Then take your favorite small toys (wood or plastic works best) and stamp them into the clay's surface, creating impressions of their shapes.

Magical hippo

Ancient Egyptian art

Look at this!

Hippopotamus figurine, *c.* 1961-1878 BCE

Not your usual pet, is it? In ancient Egypt, people liked to have a blue hippopotamus figurine with them when they were buried. They believed it would help them to be reborn magically.

Discuss this!

This statuette is covered with lotus flowers. The lotuses represent not only the river where hippos live but also the idea of life and rebirth in ancient Egypt.

- What is your favorite flower? If lotuses represent life and rebirth, what does your favorite flower represent?
- Did you know that the ancient Egyptians thought the hippo was one of the most dangerous animals? Does this hippo look scary to you?
- What's the usual color of a hippo? Do you like it in blue?

Give it a try!

Make your own magical animal figurine like an ancient Egyptian.

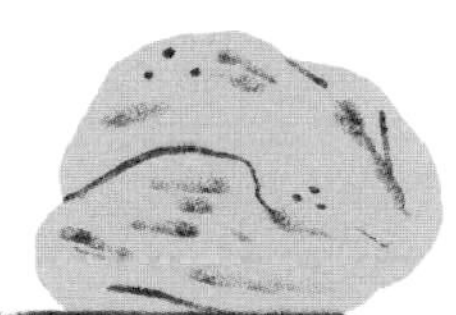

You will need:

- Air-dry clay
- A bowl of water
- Blue and white washable paint-mix it together to make your favorite shade of blue
- Brushes
- Black pen

1

Start by splitting off a ball of clay. Shape it into a cylinder: this is your magical hippo's body.

2

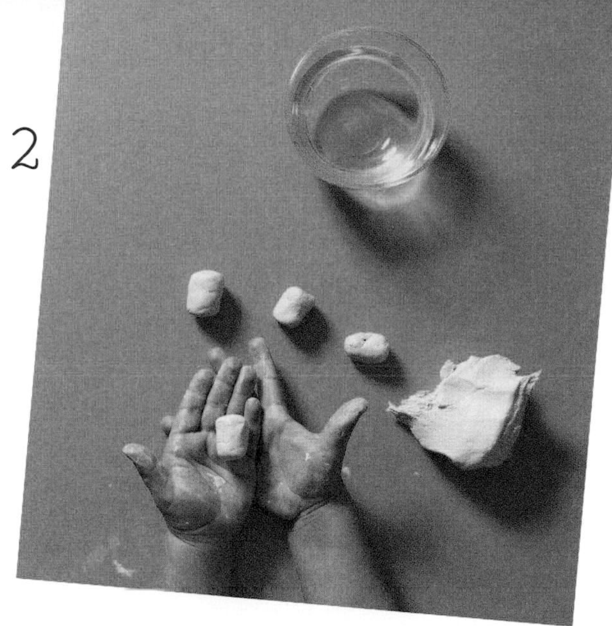

Next, work four small pieces of clay to make four little legs. They should roughly be the shape of short cylinders.

3

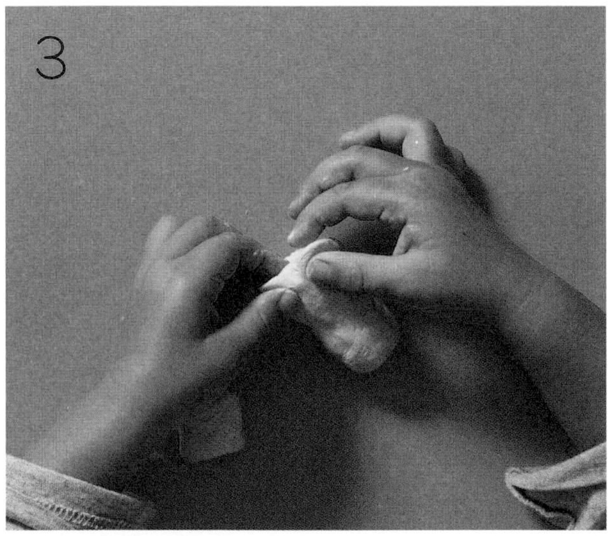

Use your last piece of clay to make the neck, which should be thicker than the leg, and to shape the head. By pinching the clay you can add two small ears.

4

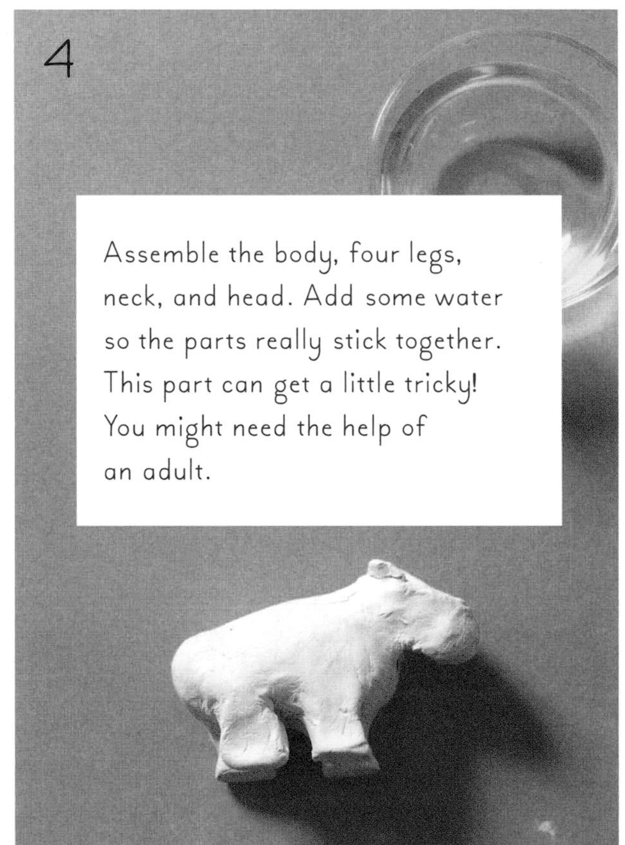

Assemble the body, four legs, neck, and head. Add some water so the parts really stick together. This part can get a little tricky! You might need the help of an adult.

Tip! Don't make the head too big—if it is too heavy for your figurine, it will make it fall over.

Let it dry–ideally overnight, but at least for a couple of hours. Once the clay is dry, you can paint it in your favorite shade of blue.

Let the paint dry. Then, using a black pen, draw the eyes, the mouth, and lotuses (or your favorite flowers) to decorate your hippo.

Ancient Egyptians loved cats. Why don't you give your hippo a companion by making your own cat figurine out of clay? According to the ancient Egyptians, your cat will bring you justice and power, too–we'll take that!

Misty landscapes

Chinese ink-wash painting

Look at this!

Fan Kuan, *Travelers by Streams and Mountains*, c. 1000 CE

This Chinese landscape painting is very big–it's more than five feet tall. It celebrates nature in all its glory. The term for "landscape painting" in Chinese (*shanshui hua*) means "mountain water painting"–you can probably guess why!

Discuss this!

Look out of the window and describe what you see. Next, look at this painting and imagine that's the view from the window–art can transport us to different times and places.

- Can you spot the travelers and the waterfall?
- Where would you walk if you were to step into this painting?
- Which season do you think it shows? What time of day?

Give it a try!

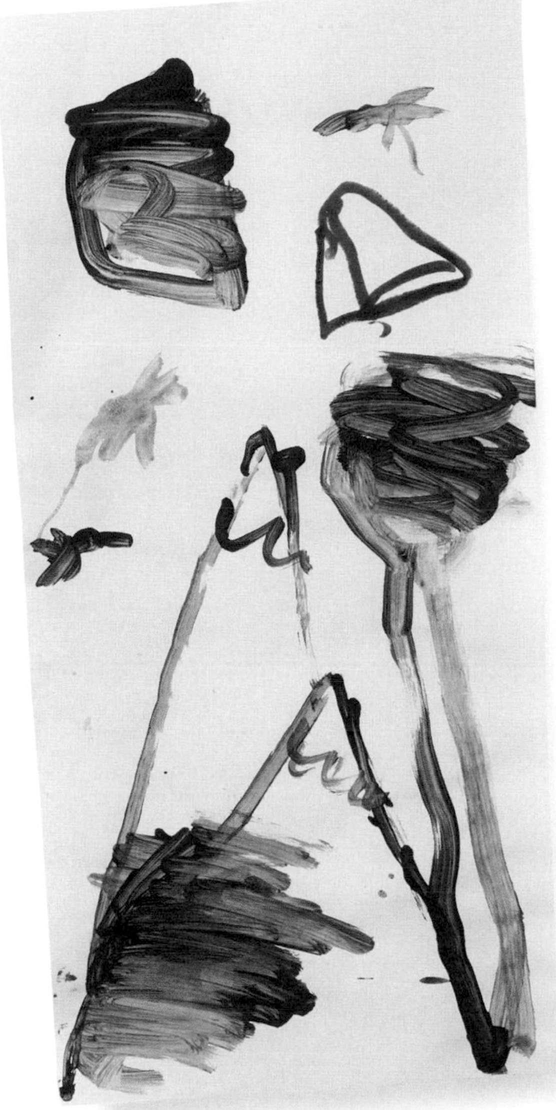

Paint your own misty landscape scene. Include water and a mountain, like a traditional Chinese landscape.

You will need:

- A scroll of paper (you can make this by sticking several sheets of paper together)
- Four bowls
- Washable black paint (or ink for older children)
- Water
- Paintbrushes
- Red pen

1

First, lay out the paper scroll. Prepare four bowls of paint with water added to make black, dark gray, gray, and light gray. Adding more water will make a lighter shade of gray.

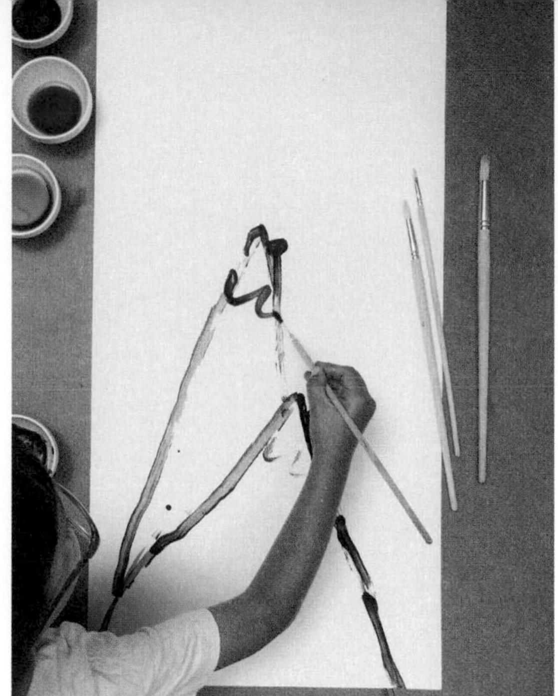

2

Imagine a beautiful mountain landscape. Use a brush to paint the outlines of your scene using the black paint.

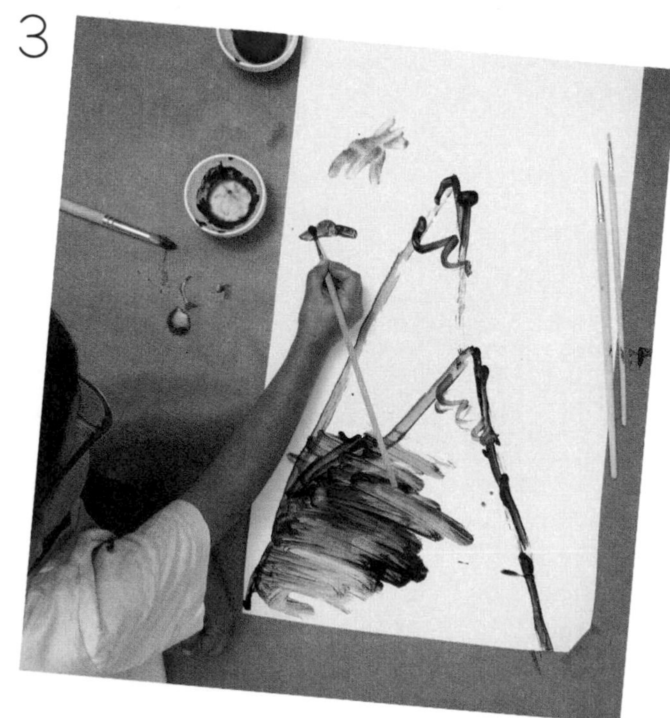

3

Use the dark-gray paint to add the textures of the mountains and trees.

Tip! It's OK not to fill up the scroll—leaving a bit of empty space makes your painting look even more dreamy and poetic.

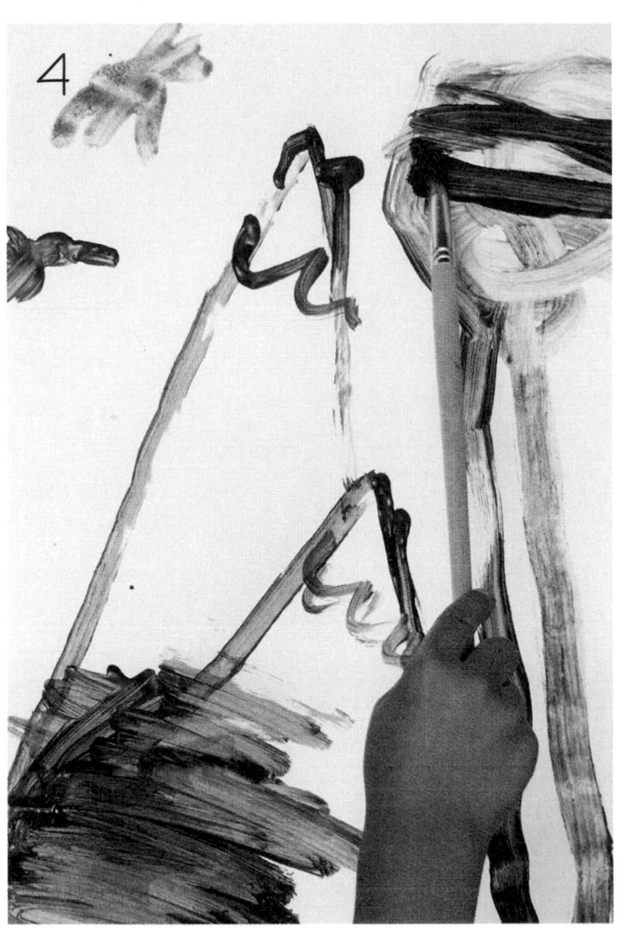

Use the lighter shades of gray paint to add features like waterfalls, rocks, and clouds. Keep going until your scene is complete.

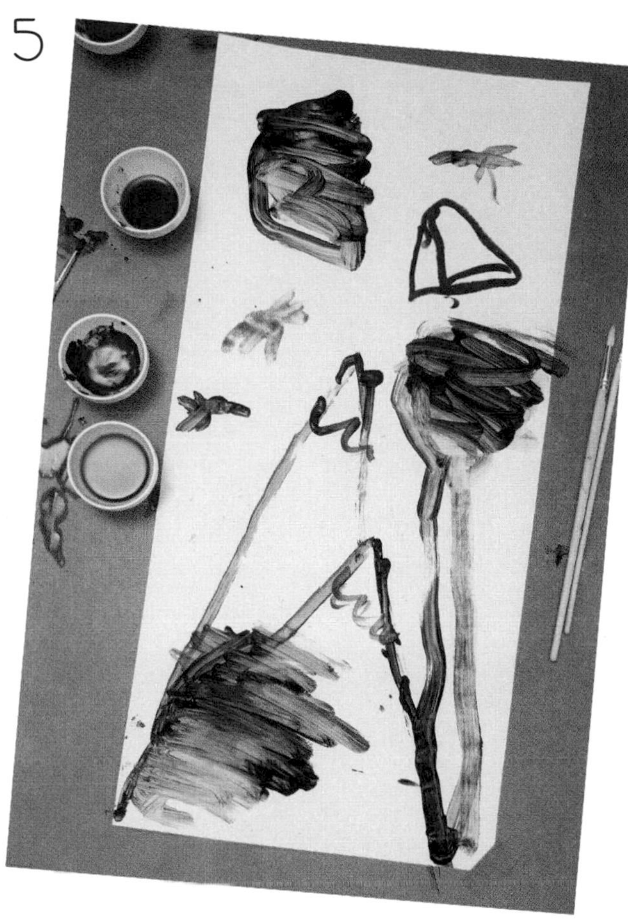

Use a red pen to sign your mini masterpiece by writing the first letter of your name in a shape like a square or triangle.

Try this!

Chinese painters were experts at calligraphy. Take a big piece of paper and use black paint and a brush to draw some curly lines and a fancy version of your name or favorite numbers.

Rainbow windows

Medieval stained glass

Look at this!

Stained-glass windows at the Sainte-Chapelle in Paris, France, 1242–48 CE

That's some window! The walls appear to be almost entirely made of stained glass. In the Upper Chapel of the Sainte-Chapelle ("Holy Chapel") in Paris, the light is magical on a sunny day. This jewel of Gothic architecture features some of the most beautiful stained glass in the world.

Discuss this!

Colored and painted glass was an important art form in medieval Europe for more than six centuries. Can you see why this type of art was popular for so long?

- Can you spot all the colors of the rainbow?
- How does it make you feel when you look at these windows? Does it make you happy?
- What do you think this place could be used for?

Give it a try!

Now it's your turn to make medieval stained glass, packed with colors.

You will need:

- Thick black paper
- Pencil
- Scissors
- Tissue paper in various colors, cut or torn into smaller pieces
- Glue
- Sticky tack or masking tape

1

On black paper, draw the shape of a gothic window, with a flat bottom and two tall, curving sides that meet in a point at the top. Draw window panes inside the frame.

2

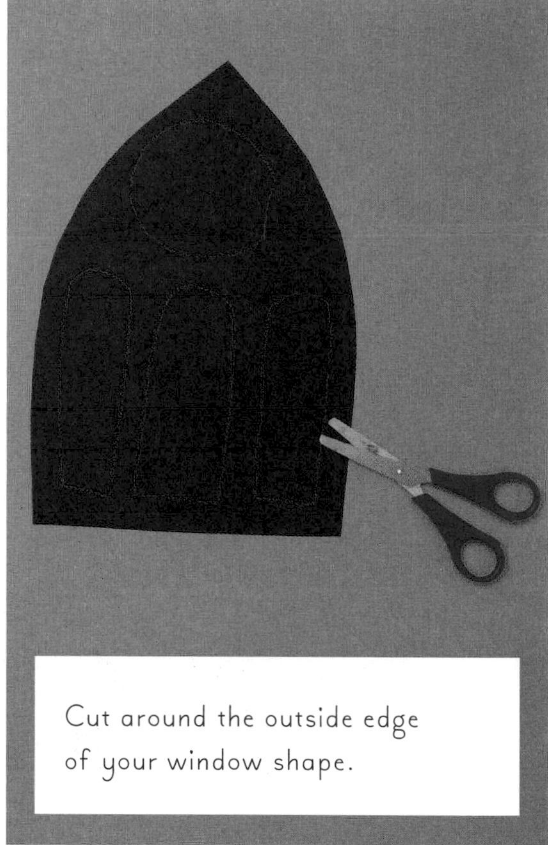

Cut around the outside edge of your window shape.

3

Next, cut holes for the window panes. (Mini artists should ask an adult for help.)

4

Take pieces of tissue paper in various sizes and colors. Place them on the back of your frame, over the holes. Make sure there are no gaps.

Glue or tape the tissue paper to the frame.

Turn it over to see your stained-glass window. You could even tape it to your real-life window, like on page 29. Admire the light shining through!

Tip! Try to put pairs of complementary colors next to each other, such as orange and blue, purple and yellow, or red and green.

Try this!

Medieval artists were experts with light. Why not try making a small lantern in stained glass? Take a glass jar and glue colorful tissue paper all over the outside of the glass. Ask an adult for help lighting a small tealight candle and place it inside to bring your lantern to life!

Mosaic faces

Aztec masks

Look at this!

Mosaic mask, 1400-1521 CE

In many pre-Columbian cultures in Mexico, masks were religious objects. This striking mask from the Aztec culture was probably worn in religious ceremonies. It is made of cedro wood and covered in turquoise mosaic. The pierced eyes are in pearl and the teeth are made of shell.

Discuss this!

That's a scary face.
Some people are alarmed by masks–
how does it make you feel when you look at this one?

- Who do you think this mask is the portrait of? A king? A god? Experts think it might be the face of Xiuhtecuhtli, (shoo-tay-*koo*-tlee) the Aztec god of fire, but we can't be sure.
- Can you name the different face parts?
- How do you think this mask might have been used?

Give it a try!

Create your own mosaic mask inspired by the Aztecs.

You will need:

- Card or construction paper
- Foam self-adhesive mosaic squares
- Pencil
- Black pen
- Scissors

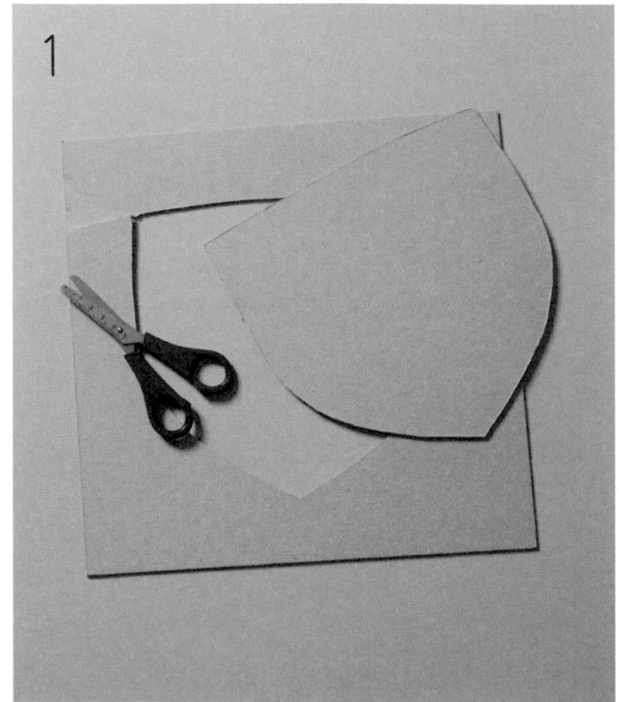

Draw the outline of a face on some card or construction paper. Carefully cut along the drawn line to cut out the mask.

Draw on eyes, a nose, and a mouth.

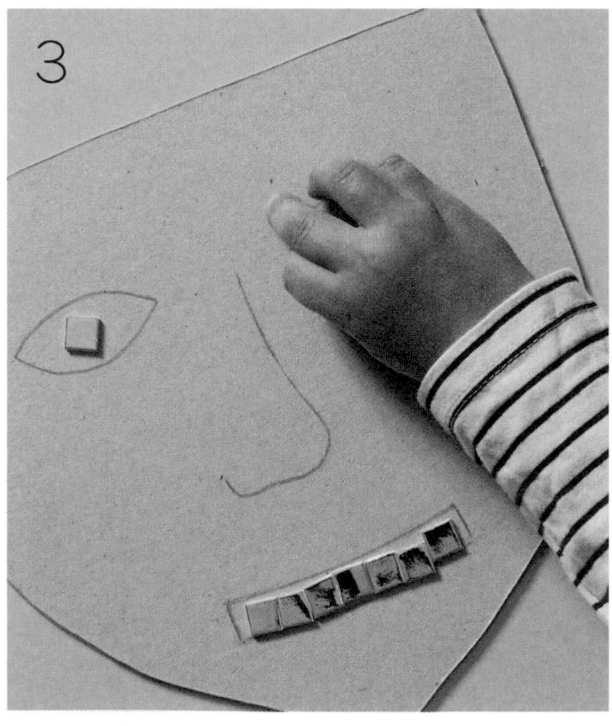

Cover the eyes and teeth in white or silver mosaic squares. To make the pointy edges of each eye, cut a square into two small triangles. Add a triangle to each side of the eye.

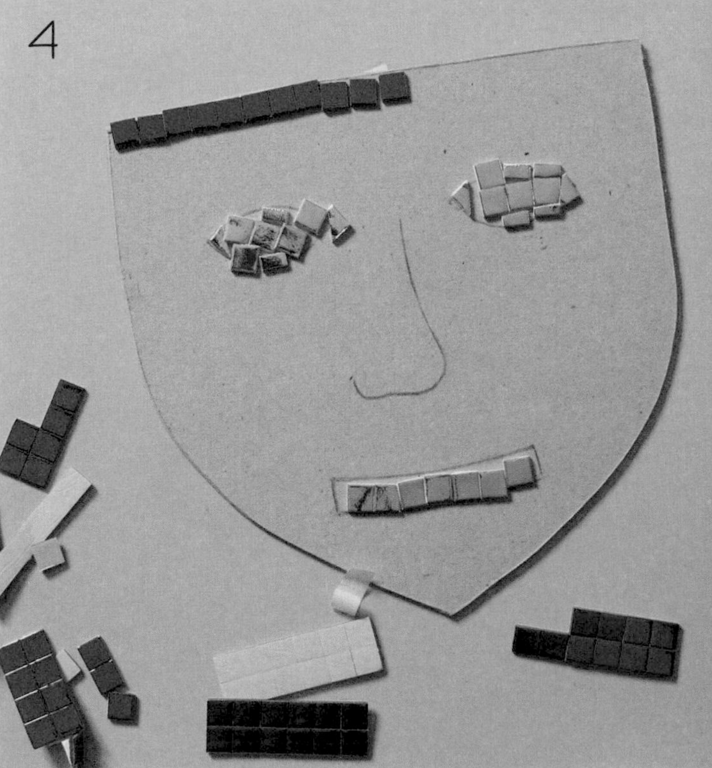

Now it's time to add colorful mosaic squares to the rest of the face.

5

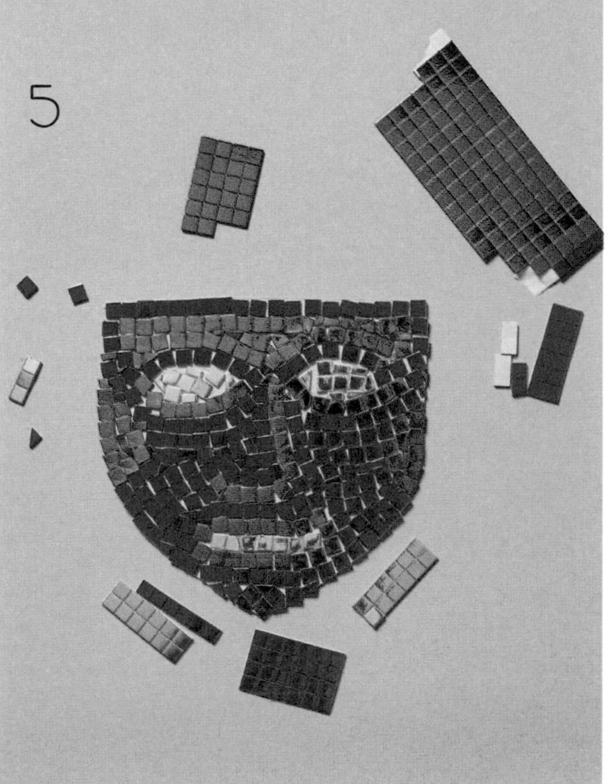

6

Keep going until you have covered the rest of the face with mosaic squares.

Use a black pen to add pupils to the eyes. Hang your mask on your door when you don't want to be disturbed!

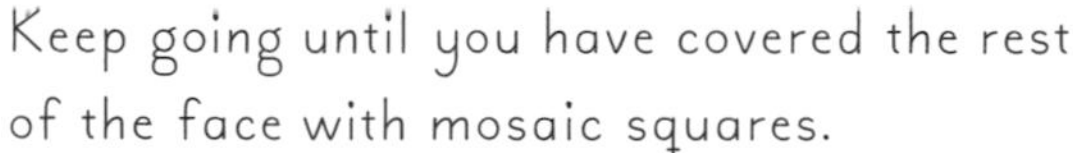

Tip! Rather than adding the mosaic squares in straight lines, try following the outline of the face and the eyes, nose and mouth.

Try this!

If you have mosaic squares left, make an Aztec double-headed serpent. Take some cardboard and draw a wiggly snake with heads on each side. Make sure to draw jaws full of sharp teeth to impress and terrify! Cut the snake out and then add mosaic squares, just like you did with your mask.

mini MODERN ARTISTS

Modern art is made by artists who shared similar aims–rejecting artistic traditions, redefining what art could be and, of course, experimenting. The artists in this section were working in the twentieth century. Lots of them are inspired by older forms of art; an important influence for lots of modern artists is the art of ancient civilizations.

Modern art pieces often have a simplicity and emotional immediacy that appeals to mini artists. From abstraction to figurative art, this section is all about exploring the visual language of shapes, forms, colors, and lines. Not all of these projects directly reference the world around us, but they can all reflect a mini artist's feelings and ideas. This can be a freeing experience and is perfect for anyone who is learning how to express themselves.

Abstract weaving

Anni Albers

Look at this!

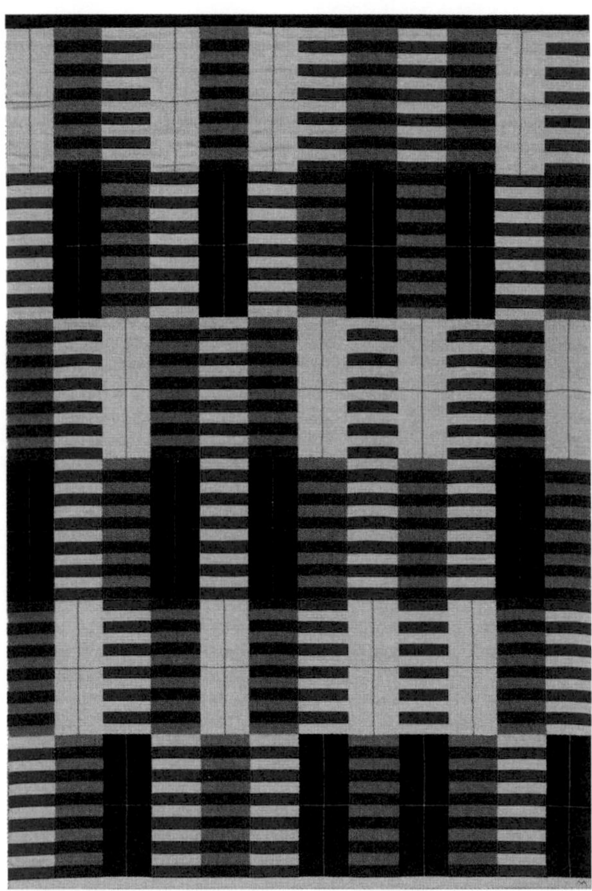

Anni Albers, *Black White Red*, 1926/1964

When textile artist Anni Albers created this abstract wall hanging, she was interested in the color combinations in the artwork. She developed this style when she studied at the Bauhaus in Germany. The Bauhaus was an art school that combined crafts and fine arts.

Discuss this!

What do you think this artwork is made of?

- Anni Albers was interested in weaving as an art form. Do you think a carpet or a curtain can be a piece of art?
- Which colors can you see in her artwork? Do you think they work well together?
- Do you like this pattern? What does it make you think of? The map of a city? Or railroad tracks, perhaps?

Give it a try!

Make your own piece of woven art using paper.

You will need:

- Colored paper (8.5x11 sheet)
- Colored paper strips (8.5x11 sheets in different colors, cut into long strips, 3/4 inch wide)
- Scissors
- Glue

1

Fold an 8.5x11 piece of paper in half horizontally. This is your "frame."

2

Cut long parallel slits into the top layer of the folded paper frame. You need to cut from the shorter edge of the paper, and leave a gap of 3/4 inch at the end.

3

Take a paper strip and weave it between the parallel slits in your frame. It should go over the first section of paper, then under the next, and so on. When you're done, gently move the strip to the end of the slits by wiggling it down.

4

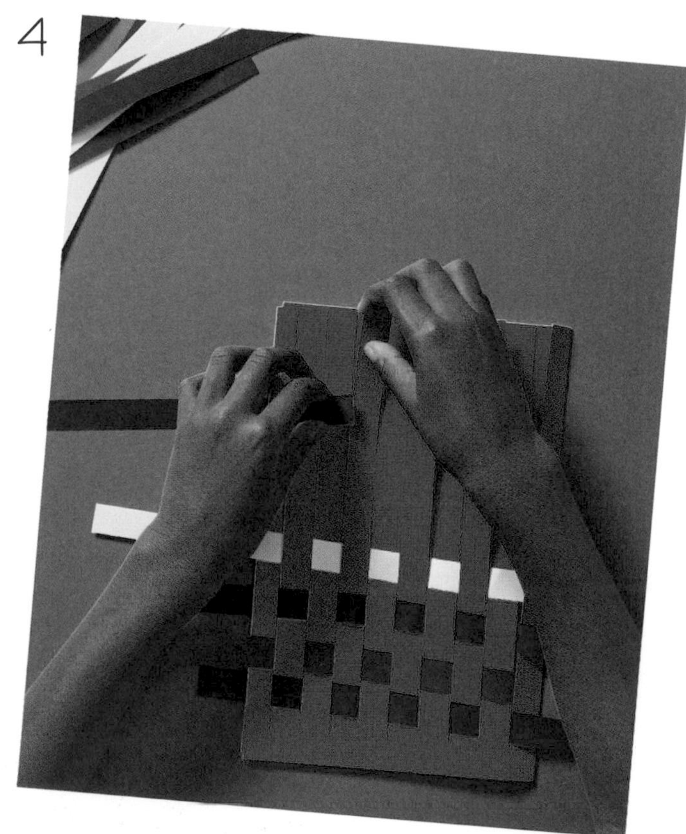

Weave more strips in–the next strip should go under where the first strip went over, and so on. Use alternating colors to make a funky pattern.

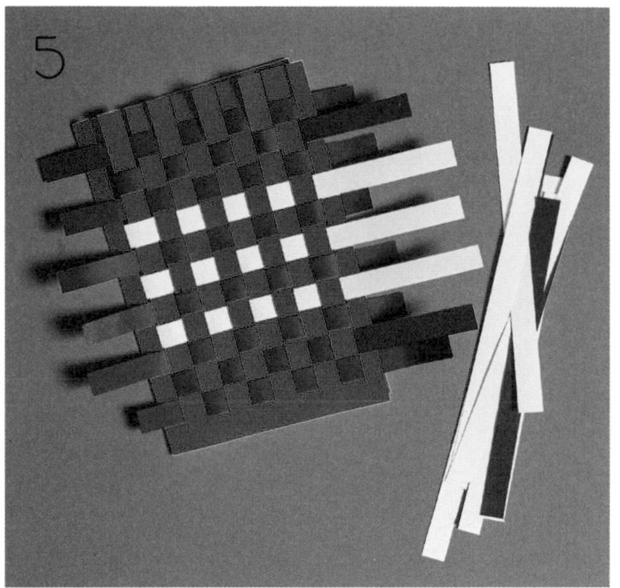

Keep adding paper strips until you have filled the slits in your frame. Add glue to the ends of each paper strip.

Fold the ends of the strips over the edges of the bottom piece of paper in your frame and stick them down. Add glue to the edges of the back layer of paper, and stick the two layers together to finish your woven artwork.

Tip! It can be helpful to draw the parallel lines on the paper using a ruler before you start cutting, to make your pattern as regular as possible.

Try this!

Now that you have learned the basics of weaving, take inspiration from Mexican weaving traditions: you can use ribbons instead of paper strips. Stick together popsicle sticks to make a frame. Tie on ribbons in parallel vertical lines, then weave ribbons over and under them in horizontal lines until you have filled the frame.

Soapy sculptures

Barbara Hepworth

Look at this!

Barbara Hepworth, *Oval sculpture, (No. 2)*, 1943

British artist Barbara Hepworth made abstract sculptures inspired by nature and the world around her. Her work was often influenced by the human body and by the landscapes and natural materials in Cornwall, England, where she had a studio and sculpture garden.

Discuss this!

Is that a giant egg with holes in it? Think about what it might be, and how it became that way. Does it look like a piece of stone that has been shaped by human hands?

- Which geometric shapes can you see?
- What do you think the sculpture could be made from?
- Do you think it's very heavy?
- Would you like to walk around it?

Give it a try!

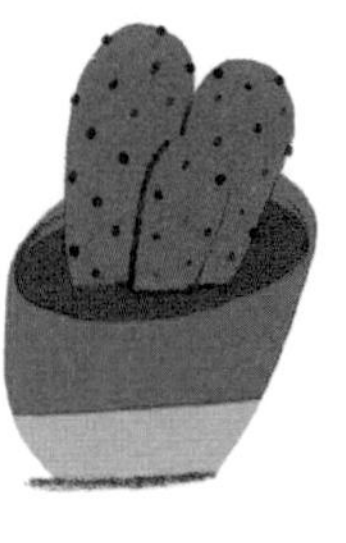

Make an abstract sculpture out of soap. Make sure to add an intriguing hole! When it's finished, you could display it with some potted plants to make a mini sculpture garden.

You will need:

- A large bar of soap
- Child-friendly clay modeling tools, or kids' silverware

1

First, carve your soap into an oval or egg-shape. Make one side flat–this will be the base.

2

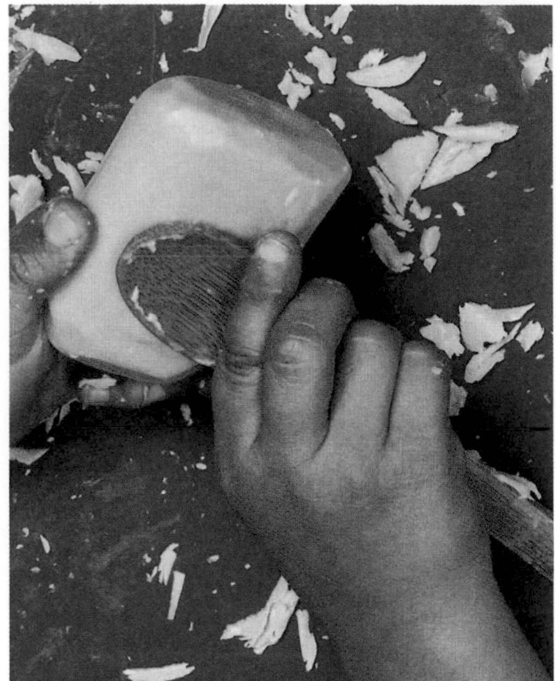

Make the oval as smooth as you can by working on the surface with your tools and your hands.

3

Carefully make one hole all the way through the middle of the soap, like a tunnel. You can hold your tool in one position and rotate it to chip away at the soap gently.

4

Use your hands to remove any rough edges and blow away the left-over soap chippings.

5

Take a step back to admire your soapy sculpture. When it's finished, keep your sculpture in a dry place–or use it to wash your hands!

Tip! Try to work very gently throughout, to avoid breaking the soap.

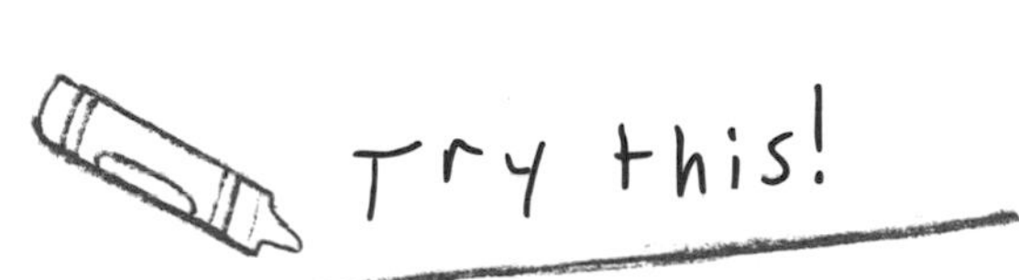

Try this!

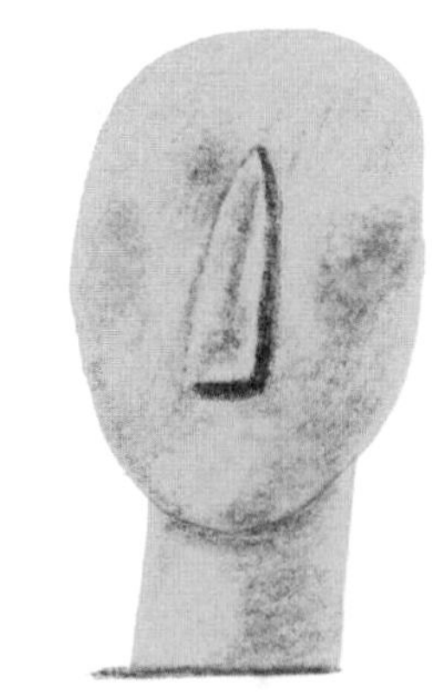

Barbara Hepworth was also inspired by "Cycladic" sculptures from ancient Greece. These were very stylized and simplified sculptures of human forms. Why not use the same soap carving technique as you used for your abstract sculpture, but this time making a simplified face?

Drip paintings

Jackson Pollock

Look at this!

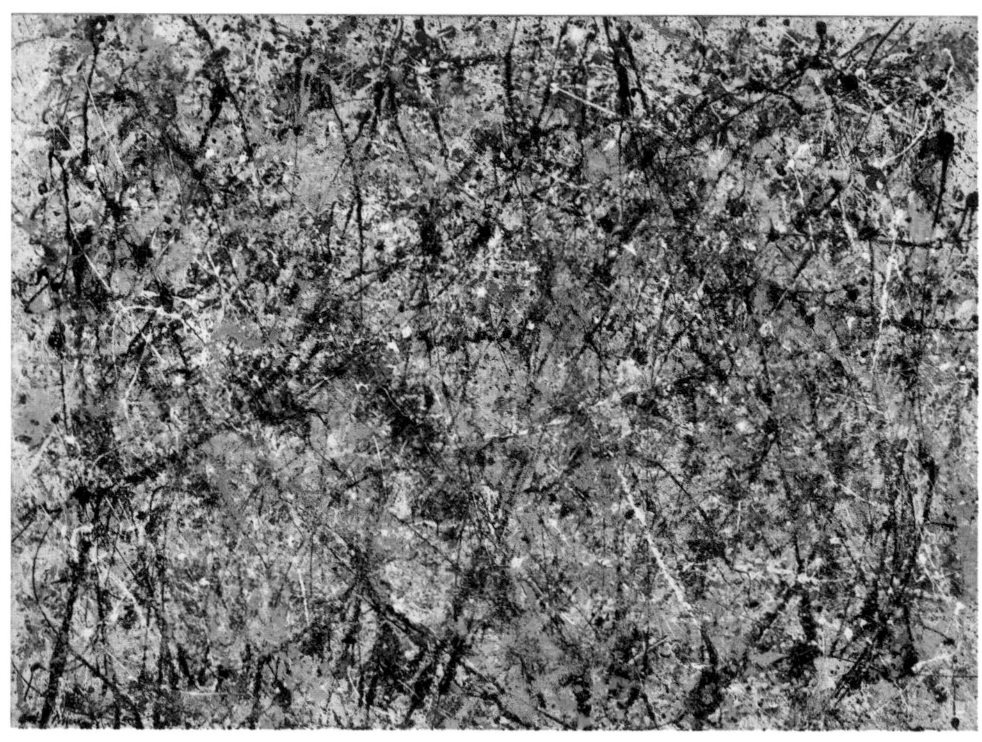

Jackson Pollock, *Number 1, 1950 (Lavender Mist)*, 1950

Pollock put his large canvases on the floor and dribbled paint across them. He moved quickly, in a technique called "action painting." He was inspired by Navajo sand painters, who create paintings for religious ceremonies by dropping colored sand onto the ground.

Discuss this!

Abstract art may seem like a sophisticated idea, but you might be surprised at how much you can "read" in an image. There are no wrong answers!

- Do you recognize anything in the painting? A face? A flower? The sun?
- Does this painting look calm to you? Scary? Angry? Sad?
- How do the colors make you feel?
- How do you think the artist made the painting?

Give it a try!

Embrace your inner abstract expressionist by trying the drip-painting technique.

You will need:

- Large sheet of white paper
- Rocks or masking tape
- Cups
- Water
- (Super) washable paint in several colors
- Paintbrushes

You will need a lot of space (and clothes you don't mind being covered in paint, just in case). Paint outside if you can!

1

Place paint in cups with a little water–it should be as thick as pancake batter. Lay out the paper and use masking tape or rocks to keep it flat.

2

Check that the paint is wet enough by dipping a paintbrush into it. It should form thick drips.

3

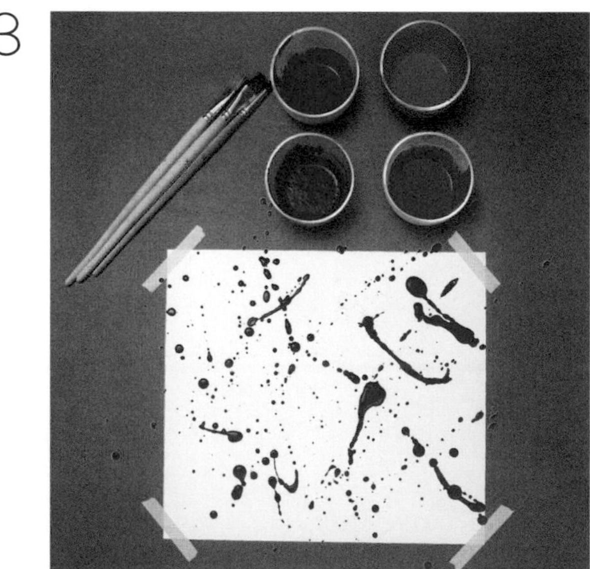

Take the cup with the darkest color of paint and tip it gently over the paper to start dripping. Make a variety of patterns including lines, circles, and curves.

4

Now choose another color. You can either drip the paint straight from the cup or use the end of a paintbrush.

5

Add as many colors as you like. Keep layering the colors and adding more drips until you feel it's finished–it can be hard to know when to stop!

6

It may take up to two days for the paint to dry. When it's dry, remove the masking tape.

Tip! Work on the floor if you can. I like to tape oil cloth to the kitchen floor, or work outside on sheets of old newspaper if the weather is warm!

Try this!

Try a similar technique but with a pencil–let's call it "action drawing." Tape some paper to a hard floor and make the pencil dance to the rhythm of your heart! You could also turn on some music to find your groove.

Surrealist creatures

Wifredo Lam

Look at this!

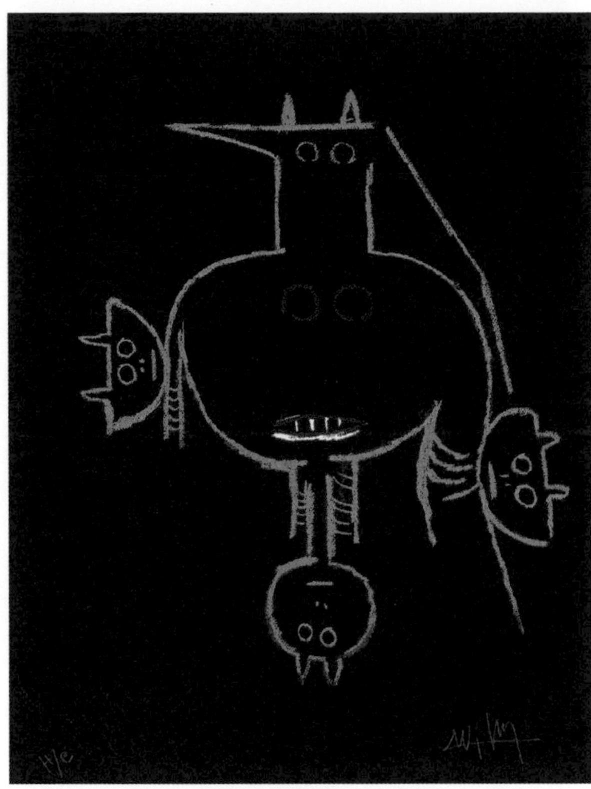

Wifredo Lam, *Untitled*, 1974

In this lithograph print, Cuban artist Wifredo Lam depicts a creature with several faces. Each of these mask-like faces represents a spirit worshipped in rituals in West Africa and in Haiti. Lam's work combines his interest in Afro-Caribbean spiritual traditions and surrealism.

Discuss this!

Wifredo Lam was fascinated with the spirits of nature and the idea of transformation.

- How many little spirits can you see in the print? Are they scary or friendly?
- How many heads, necks, and bodies is this creature made of?
- Does it remind you of a creature you might meet in a story or a dream?
- If you were not a human, which animal or plant would you be?

Give it a try!

Print your own surrealist creature inspired by the world of Wifredo Lam.

You will need:

- Foam sheet
- Sharp pencil
- Black washable paint
- Plate or paint tray
- Rolling brush
- Sheets of plain paper
- Red pen or crayon

1

Imagine a magical creature with lots of heads and lots of personality. Use a sharp pencil to draw your creature on a foam sheet.

2

Pour black paint on a plate or paint tray. Use the rolling brush to cover your creature in black paint. Try to do it evenly in a thick layer. The thicker the paint, the darker the print will be.

3

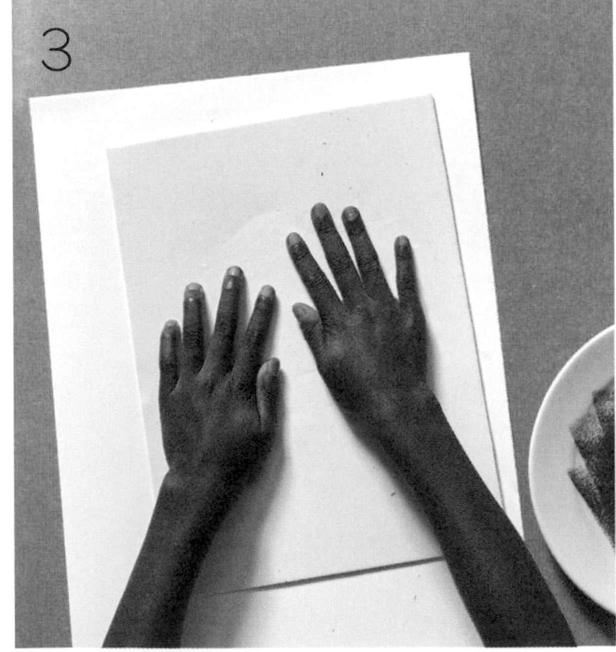

Transfer your design by applying the foam sheet to a sheet of white paper. Press the foam sheet onto the paper for up to ten seconds.

4

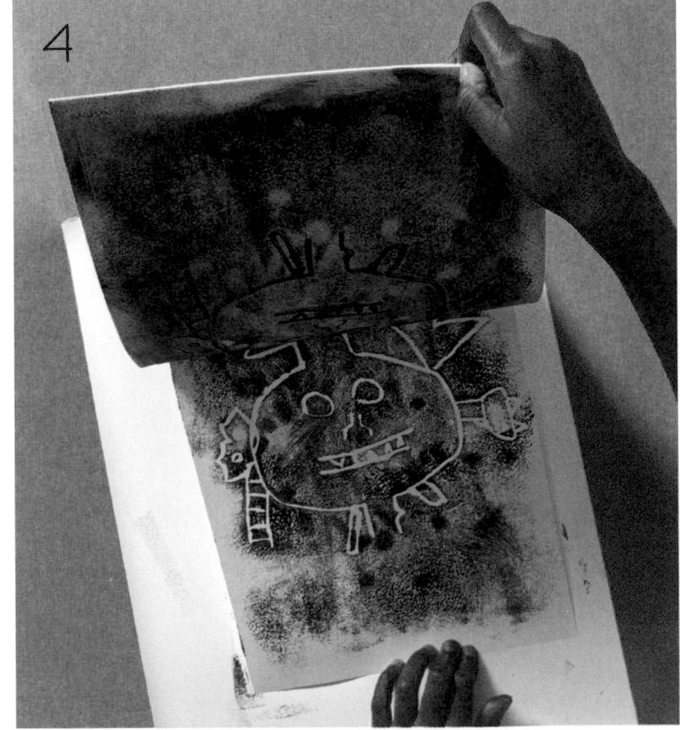

Carefully remove the foam sheet and let your print dry for a few minutes.

Use a red pen or crayon to add more details to your creature, like eyes, noses, and mouths.

Sign and number your print. Then you can make another one!

Tip! After you have made your print, you can press the foam sheet on another sheet of paper without reapplying any paint to make a second print.

Try this!

Another way to make a print is by using stamps. To make your own homemade stamps, cut various shapes out of foam sheets and glue them on pieces of cardboard. Dip them in paint and press them on paper to make prints. Start with simple shapes.

Colorful cutouts

Henri Matisse

Look at this!

Henri Matisse, *The Sorrow of the King*, 1952

Henri Matisse was known for his colorful oil paintings, but he also invented a technique of "painting with scissors." He cut out pieces of colorful paper that were then glued onto large sheets of paper. In the 1940s, Matisse became a wheelchair user, which made it tricky for him to use paints and brushes, but he was still able to create art by "painting with scissors." These paper cutouts are a highlight of Matisse's career.

Discuss this!

Can you see any characters in this artwork? Who might they be? Here, Matisse shows himself next to the figures of a musician and a woman to celebrate the soothing power of music.

- What do you think these figures are doing?
- Who looks sad and who do you think is happy?
- How many colors has Matisse used?
- What's your favorite detail in the painting?

Give it a try!

Create your own cutout scene in stunning colors and shapes.

You will need:

- Paper in a variety of colors
- Scissors
- Glue

Take four colorful pieces of paper, and cut out a simple geometric shape from each of them. Triangles, squares, and rectangles work well.

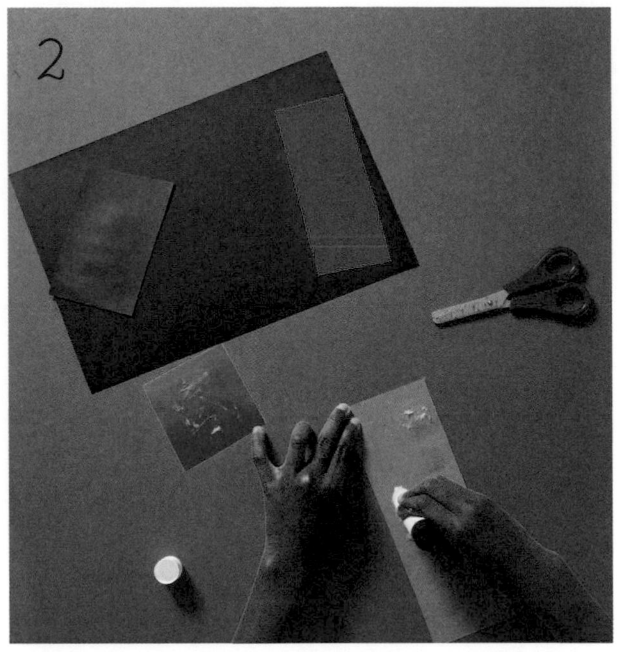

Choose a different-colored piece of paper for your background. Glue the geometric shapes to the background.

Take four more colors of paper. Cut out four large organic shapes, like leaves, plants, stains, or splotches.

Try placing your organic shapes in different positions on top of your background paper. Once you are pleased with your composition, stop and glue them in place.

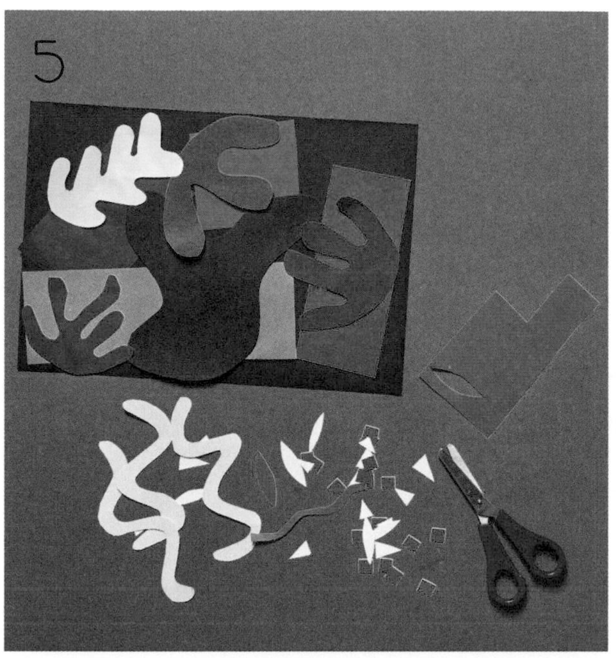

Cut smaller elements from the remaining scraps of colored paper. Try funky shapes like ziz-zags, drops, spots, and tiny triangles.

Glue the funky decorative pieces on top of your cutout artwork to complete it.

Tip! Choose a dark color such as black or navy blue as the background, and use light colors such as white or yellow for the final decorative elements.

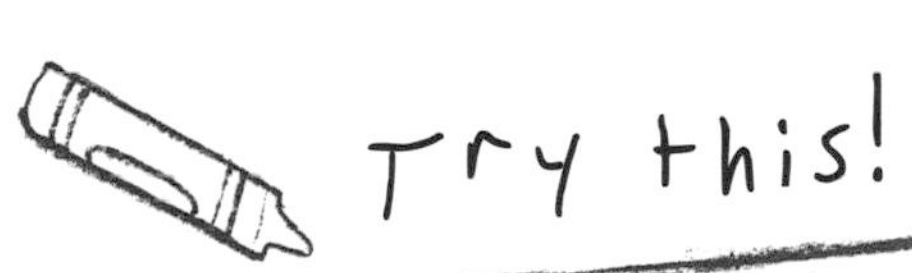

Make another collage from pieces of magazines and newspapers, rather than plain paper. Cut out between ten and twenty elements from printed pictures–body parts and facial features work particularly well! Next, glue them together on a piece of paper to make a collage.

Monochrome textures

Louise Nevelson

Look at this!

Louise Nevelson, *Total Totality II*, 1959-68

American artist Louise Nevelson made her abstract sculptures from bits and pieces she found on the streets of New York. Once assembled, she made the sculpture into a whole by painting it all in the same color of paint.

Discuss this!

Did you know that the trinkets and knickknacks you collect during the day can be made into art? When foraged bits and pieces are combined into an artwork, it is called "assemblage."

- What are we looking at? A painting? A sculpture? Or a little of both?
- How many elements can you see? Doesn't it look like the inside of a drawer?
- Can you recognize any shapes or objects?
- Are they organized carefully or thrown together?

Give it a try!

Make a simple assemblage project out of cardboard. If you like, make several in different colors! Feel free to add small objects if you're feeling adventurous.

You will need:

- Cardboard (as many different textures as you can find: boxes, egg cartons, and fruit packaging work well)
- Scissors
- Glue
- Washable paint
- Paintbrushes
- 2 small bowls

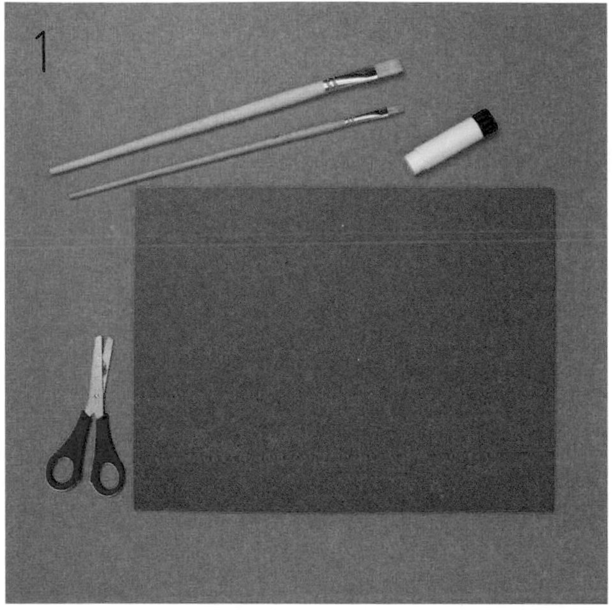

Cut a large rectangular piece of cardboard. This is your surface.

Cut and tear pieces of cardboard into various sizes and shapes. Try to make as many different shapes as you can and include lots of textures–be creative!

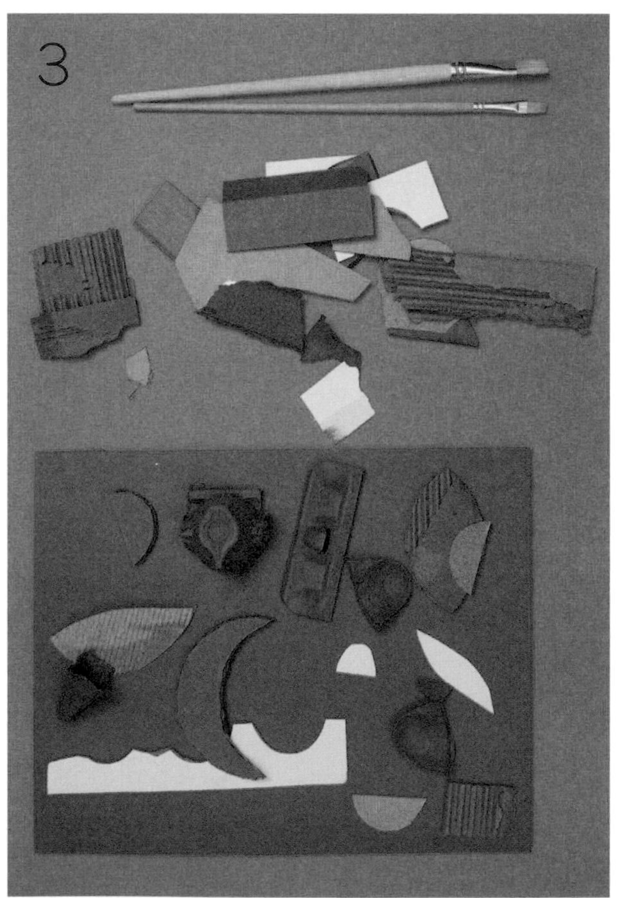

Place the smaller cardboard pieces on your cardboard surface. Move them around to create a composition you like.

Use glue to fix all your pieces of cardboard to the cardboard surface.

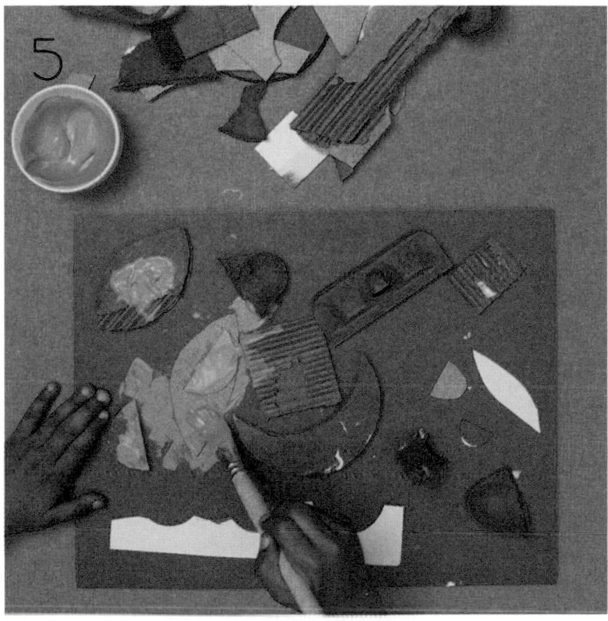

When the glue is dry, paint the entire artwork in your favorite color.

6

Make sure the whole surface is covered with paint for maximum impact. Your monochrome assemblage is complete!

Tip! When making your cardboard shapes, try tearing off the top layer of card to show the wavy "corrugated" part underneath—it will add texture!

Try this!

Did you like assembling pieces of cardboard? Then you will love assembling bits and pieces! Louise Nevelson's favorite objects included wood scraps and waste from the street. What will yours be? We love puzzle pieces, bottle tops, corks, chopsticks, and keys! It's exactly the same technique (sticking items to cardboard), just with different materials.

Mini tropical garden

Hélio Oiticica

Look at this!

Hélio Oiticica, *Tropicália*, 1966-67

In this immersive installation by Hélio Oiticica, the floor is covered in sand and has a path flanked by tropical plants. There are poems on wooden boards and structures in bright colors.

Discuss this!

Would you like to enter *Tropicália*? Hélio Oiticica's intention was to make viewers actively engage with art.

- What would you like to do first if you walked through this artwork? Would you read the poems or play in the structures?
- What is a path usually made of?
- How many tropical plants (or animals) can you name?
- Do you know a poem by heart, or can you remember a few lines from your favorite book?

Give it a try!

Make your own tropical installation inspired by Hélio Oiticica.

You will need:

- A tray or a very large dish
- Sand
- Gravel or pebbles
- Miniature indoor plants
- Colorful construction paper
- Tape
- Pens

1

Cover your tray in sand. Add a winding path made of pebbles or gravel.

2

Place your miniature indoor plants along the path.

3

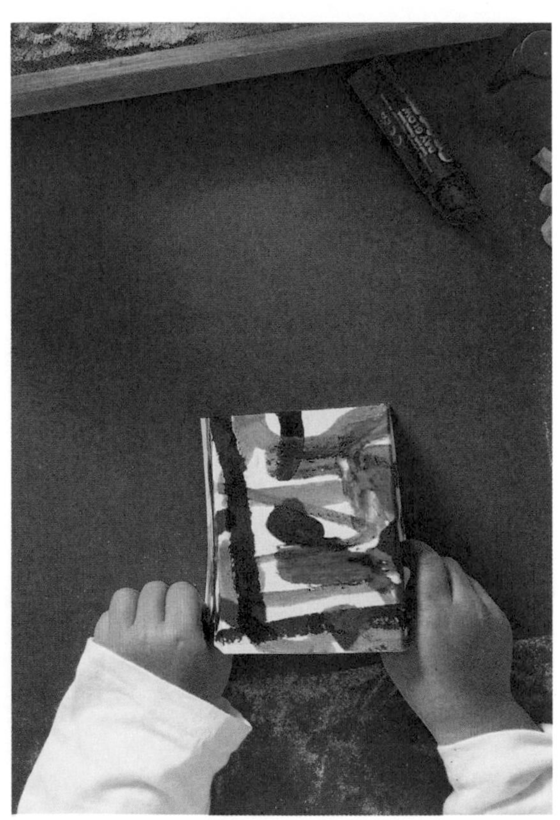

Make a few "structures" by folding colorful construction paper in the shape of towers. Use tape to secure them if needed. You can draw on them first if you want!

4

Write a poem or a few lines of your favorite book on one of the structures.

5

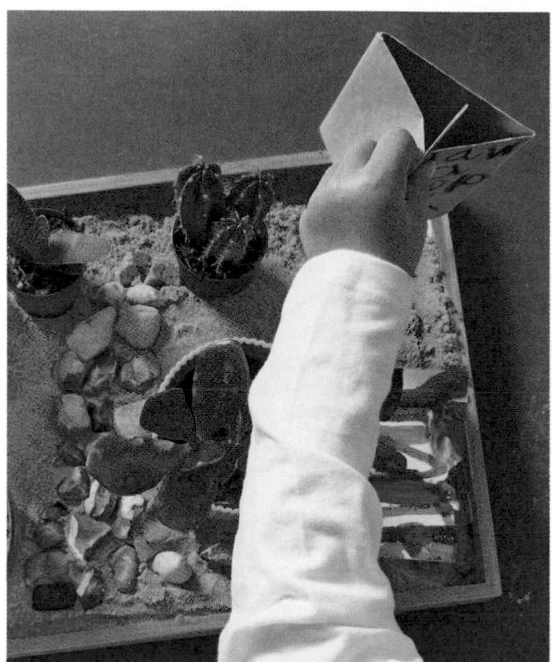

Find a good place for your structures on the tray. If you press them into the sand, they will stand by themselves.

6

Admire your installation. You can rearrange your plants and structures until you are pleased with your composition.

Tip! Be aware that cacti are spiky! Handle them with care. Add a little pond if you wish by adding a small bowl of water.

Try this!

If you are inspired by Hélio Oiticica, make an installation that encourages people to get involved. Join forces with some friends to make a life-size *Tropicália* in a garden, a park or your playground. You can each bring plants, cushions, and poems to read together.

mini
CONTEMPORARY
ARTISTS

Artists who have been creating since the early 1960s like to think big! Street art, installation art, land art, and performance art have all become popular forms of expression. Looking at contemporary art will encourage mini artists to explore big ideas when it comes to making art of their own.

In the last fifty years, the art world has become more diverse–there are as many ways to see the world as there are artists out there. Inspired by the most creative artists working today, mini artists will understand art as a way to reflect their opinion, ideas, and style. Contemporary artists tackle important issues such as racial stereotypes, waste, ecology, diversity, and identity. While the subjects can be serious, the treatment is often playful, fun, and engaging. Looking at their work is a great way to grasp the visual potential of art as well as its political power.

Street art musicians

Jean-Michel Basquiat

Look at this!

Jean-Michel Basquiat, *Trumpet*, 1984

Jean-Michel Basquiat has used bright colors to make this expressive portrait of a jazz musician. Basquiat's art often references Black history, street art, and pop culture.

Discuss this!

Basquiat started his career as a graffiti artist in New York in the 1980s. Could you tell from looking at this artwork?

- How loud do you think the musician is playing their trumpet?
- Can you spot any other accessories? How about Basquiat's trademark: the three-point crown?
- Can you read the words that are written on the painting? It looks like they've been crossed out. Which words would you include?

Give it a try!

Create an expressive portrait inspired by Jean-Michel Basquiat's trumpet player.

You will need:

- Paint sticks (or oil pastels)
- 11x17 white paper
- 8.5x11 black paper
- Small scraps of paper
- Scissors
- Glue
- Black pencil

1

Use your paint sticks or oil pastels to cover a sheet of white paper with five zones of different colors.

2

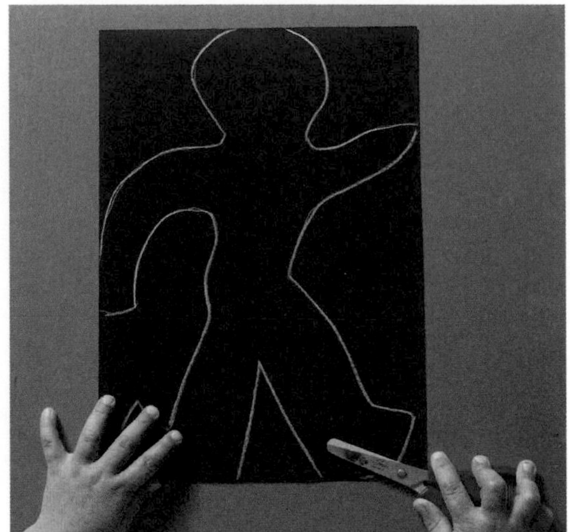

Next, draw the outline of a person on a sheet of black paper. Cut out the figure and keep the paper scraps to one side.

3

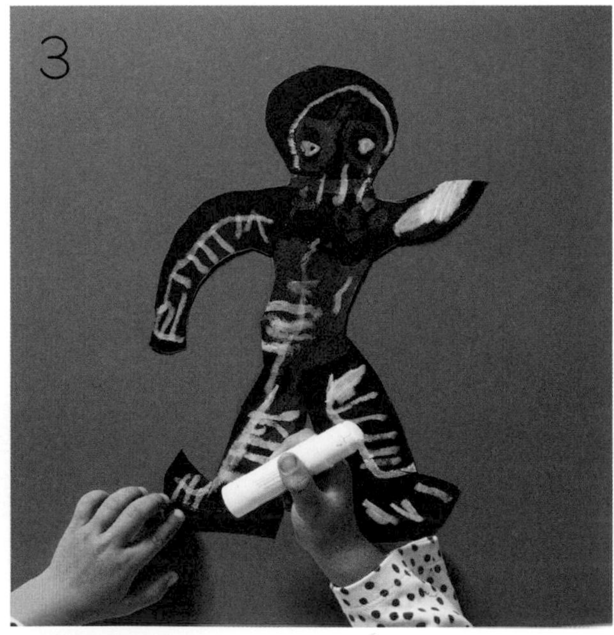

Use a white paint stick to add details and facial features to your portrait. Then draw their skeleton, like an X-ray. Add a heart using a red paint stick.

4

Glue your figure on top of the colorful white paper.

What sort of person is your portrait of? Think of a few words that they might use, for example a musician might use words like "rhythm" or "sound." Use a black pencil to write them on scraps of paper.

Stick your words on your finished portrait. Cross them out if you like, just like Basquiat, Now you can display your finished street art portrait on a wall.

Tip! Choose bright colors for the background, such as red, orange, pink, or yellow. This will help your portrait and writing to stand out.

Try this!

Another way to make street art is to use chalks and cover pavements with your art. Pick three jumbo chalks and head outside. Ask your friends to join in to draw their favorite animals!

Recycled monsters

Tony Cragg

Look at this!

Tony Cragg, *New Figuration*, 1985

To make this artwork, Tony Cragg used plastic objects that had washed up along the banks of a river. He plays with shapes to see how they can affect our ideas and emotions.

Discuss this!

This artwork is a wall arrangement–the feet of the squiggly figure are touching the floor. What do you think the sculpture is made of? What is unusual about it?

- Can you name (and point at) some body parts?
- Can you spot some recognizable objects?
- What is this person doing? Are they dancing or growing?

Give it a try!

Make your own arrangement of everyday objects to create a friendly pet monster.

You will need:

- Around 50 colorful toys and everyday objects from around the house-pick 5 colors and aim to find 10 objects in each color
- A flat floor at least ten square feet, like a corner of your yard or living room

1

First, collect fifty small objects and toys from around your home. Choose a space to work in–make sure that you have room to finish your artwork without furniture or plants getting in the way.

2

Sort the objects into piles of each color–one pile for orange, another for red, another for green, etc.

3

Choose a color. Move the objects around to form your monster's head.

4

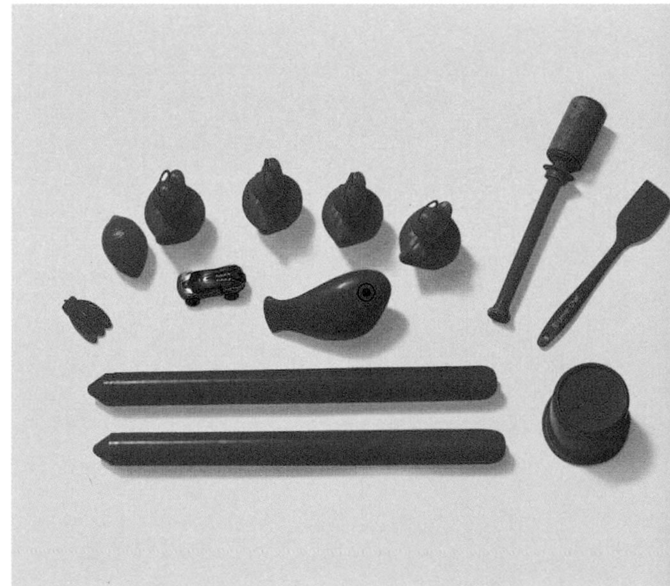

Now choose a color for the monster's body. The last three colors will form its tail and two legs.

5

You might need to stand on a chair to see the whole composition. Keep moving the objects around until you've used them all and your monster is finished. Take a picture of your creature!

Tip!

Using different colors for different body parts will help make sure your artwork has maximum visual impact!

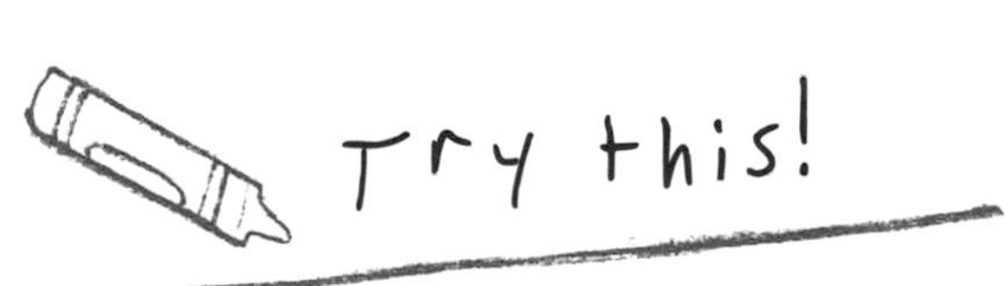

Try this!

Instead of arranging toys on the floor, make a longer-lasting artwork using recycled garbage. First, collect plenty of small pieces of plastic-bottle caps, old toothbrushes, buttons, or pieces of broken plastic toys are all good for this. Separate them by color, then draw a shape on a piece of cardboard-simple shapes such as a moon, star or heart are best. Now arrange the plastic pieces inside the shape. When you're happy with the design, glue them into place.

Floating pier

Christo and Jeanne-Claude

Look at this!

Christo and Jeanne-Claude, *The Floating Piers*, Lake Iseo, Italy, 2016

We are looking from above! This picture is a photograph of a temporary, site-specific work of art by Christo and Jeanne-Claude, installed in 2016 at Lake Iseo, near Brescia, Italy.

Discuss this!

The artwork has been installed on water: it's so big that people can even walk on it. In fact, it's two miles long! Can you imagine how long it would take to make an artwork that big?

- Can you see any houses on the island? What about people on the pier? Look closer, they are tiny!
- Where do you think the photographer was when they took the picture?
- Would you like to walk on the water?

Give it a try!

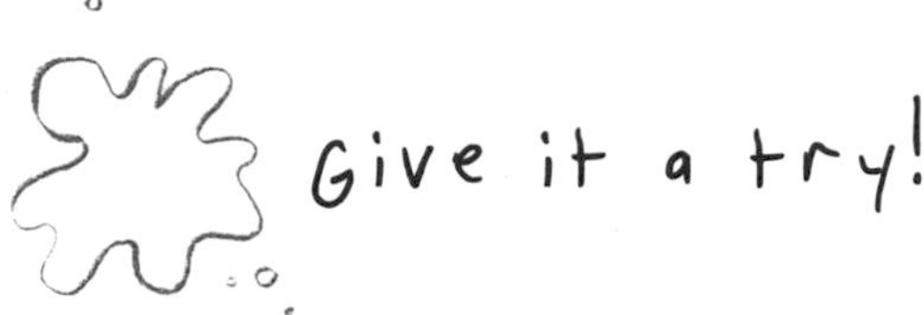

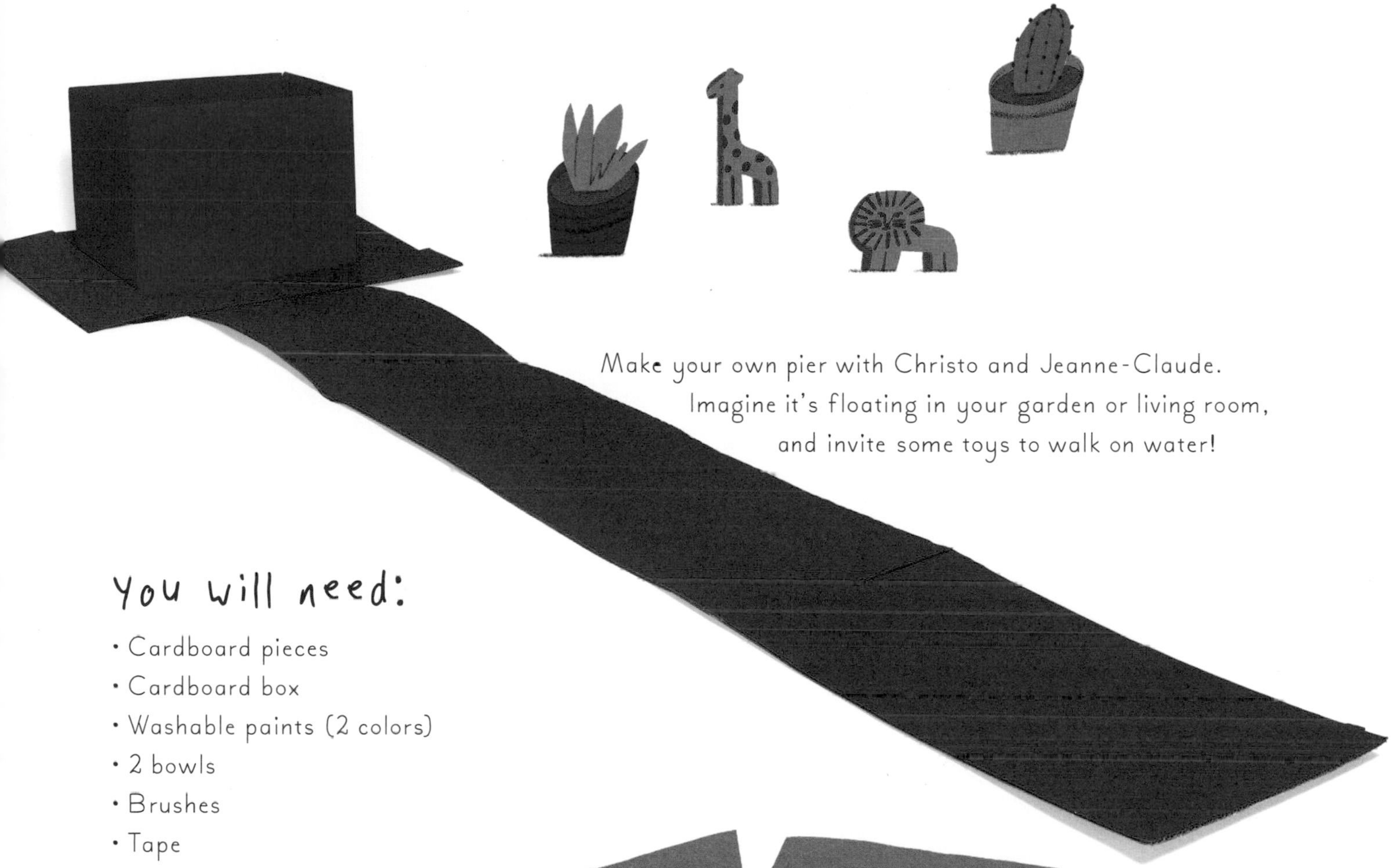

Make your own pier with Christo and Jeanne-Claude. Imagine it's floating in your garden or living room, and invite some toys to walk on water!

You will need:

- Cardboard pieces
- Cardboard box
- Washable paints (2 colors)
- 2 bowls
- Brushes
- Tape

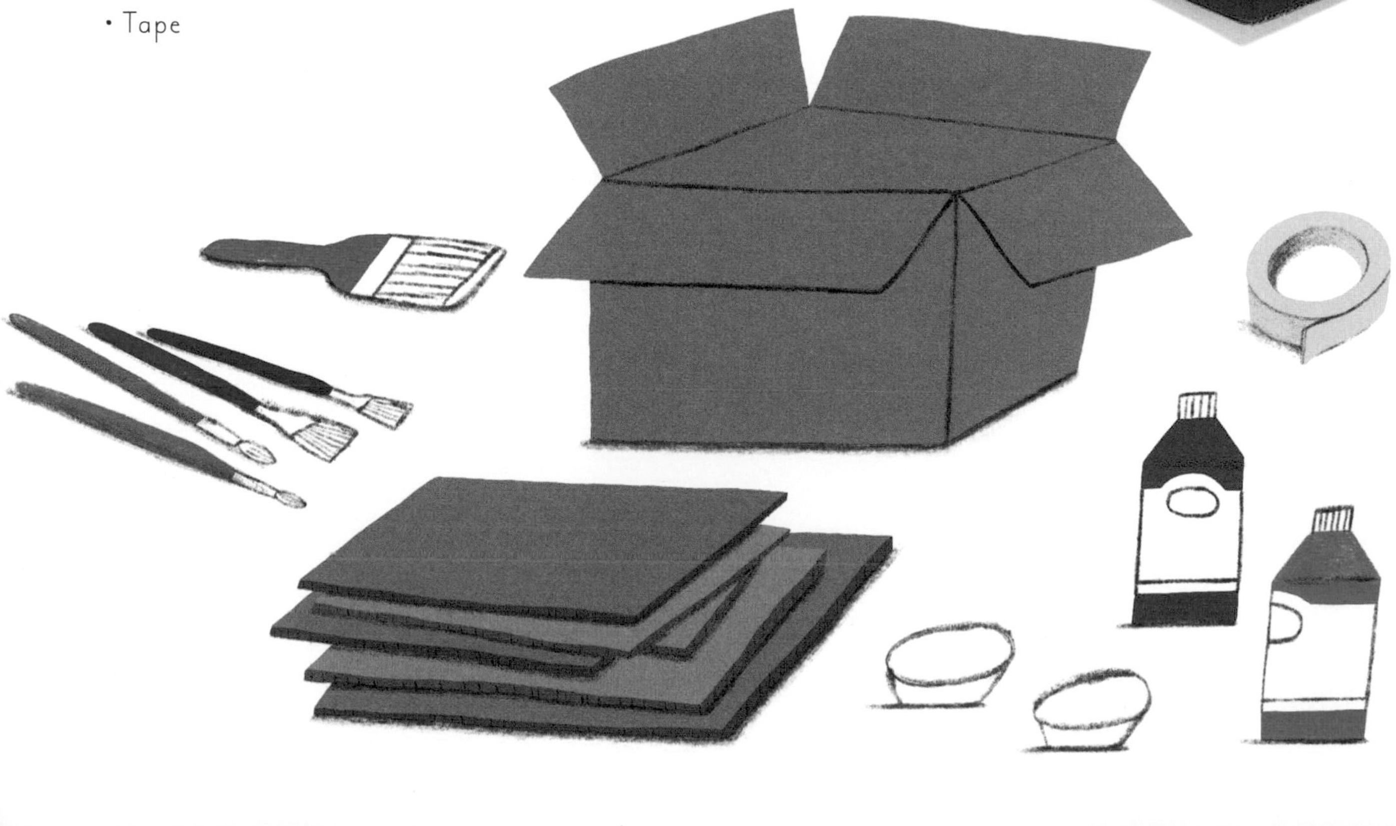

1

Use tape to stick together various pieces of cardboard to create a very long pier.

2

Pour your favorite color paint in a bowl and paint your cardboard pier.

3

Next, paint a cardboard box to make your island–preferably in a different color for contrast. Let your pier and your island dry.

4

Place your pier so that it leads up to your island, then ask an adult for help cutting out pieces of the pier to add a walkway around the island.

5

Stick your pier, island, and walkway together with tape, and enjoy! Maybe you could invite some of your favorite toys for a stroll?

Tip! Super-bright colors make a super-striking island and pier!

Try this!

Christo and Jeanne-Claude once wrapped an entire bridge in fabric. The installation at the Pont-Neuf Bridge in Paris attracted three million visitors! Why don't you find some fabric or crepe paper and tape and use them to make your own installation by wrapping up a chair, a lamp, or some books?

Nature art

Andy Goldsworthy

Look at this!

Who needs paints and brushes when you have materials found in nature? Sculptor Andy Goldsworthy's favorite art materials include stones and leaves. Here, he plays with contrast between brightly colored leaves to create a dramatic shape with a black hole at its center.

Andy Goldsworthy, *Rowan leaves laid around a hole*, 1987

Discuss this!

Goldsworthy uses his art to refer to the passing of the seasons and the cycle of life. Land art is ephemeral, which means it will change with time and eventually disappear.

- In which season of the year do you think the artist made *Rowan Leaves and Hole*?
- Are the leaves the same shape? The same color?
- Where do you think the hole in the middle leads to? What is it made of?

Give it a try!

Make a piece of land art inspired by Andy Goldsworthy.

You will need:

- Leaves (red, brown, and yellow in the autumn, or various shades of green in the spring)
- Chalk or pencil and a big piece of paper, or a sandy beach

1

Gather at least fifty leaves. Aim to collect them in a range of different colors.

2

Order the leaves into piles arranged by color. Arrange them from darkest to lightest.

3

If you're at the beach, draw the shape of a spiral by dragging your finger through the sand. Elsewhere, you can use chalk to draw the spiral on the ground if you're outside. If you're inside, draw the spiral using a pen on paper.

4

Place the leaves around the swirls of the spiral, starting from the center. Arrange them from the lightest to the darkest.

5

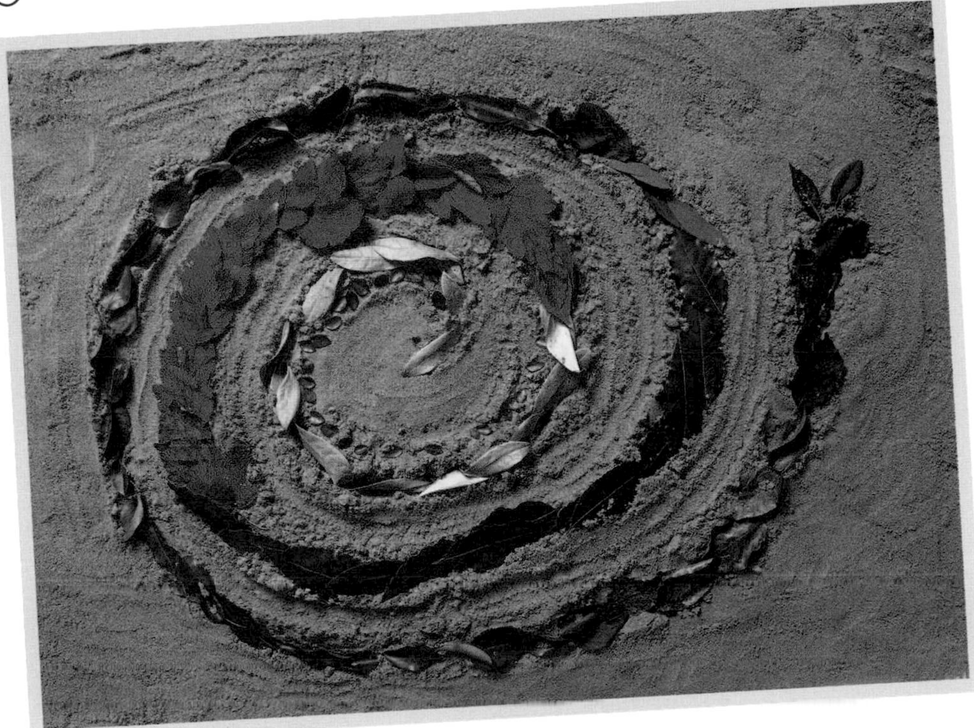

If you don't feel like making an abstract artwork, you can use leaves to add a head to turn your spiral into a snail. Remember to take a picture when you're done—land art isn't meant to last.

Tip! If you can't find any leaves, lots of round stones in various shades of gray will work well.

Try this!

Andy Goldsworthy makes magnificent ice sculptures. Forage for natural items like berries, flowers, and leaves. Put them in a plastic container, and cover them with water. Tie a piece of string into a loop and drape it over the edge of the container, with one end in the water. Place the container in the freezer overnight, then use the string to hang your ice sculpture.

Soft sculptures

Mrinalini Mukherjee

Look at this!

A soft sculpture? Mrinalini Mukherjee has chosen a very unusual material for sculpting: instead of marble or wood, she uses natural fiber. Her art is inspired by nature.

Mrinalini Mukherjee, *Aranyani*, 1996

Discuss this!

What does this sculpture represent? Mukherjee's art is neither representational nor abstract. Viewers will see different things in her work. What can you see? A sleepy volcano? A door to the underworld?

- Which skill do you think is needed to make an artwork like this? Carving or weaving?
- Which natural shapes and creatures do you like best? Name three of them, like clouds, shells, and spiders.
- How do these colors make you feel? Which colors would you use to represent nature?

Give it a try!

Make your own woven elephant sculpture, inspired by Mrinalini Mukherjee.

You will need:

- Cardboard
- Pencil
- Scissors
- Glue
- Yarn in 3 colors
- Felt squares

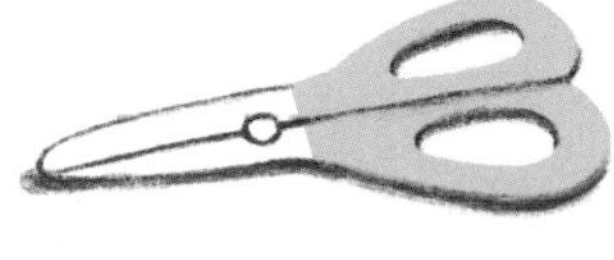

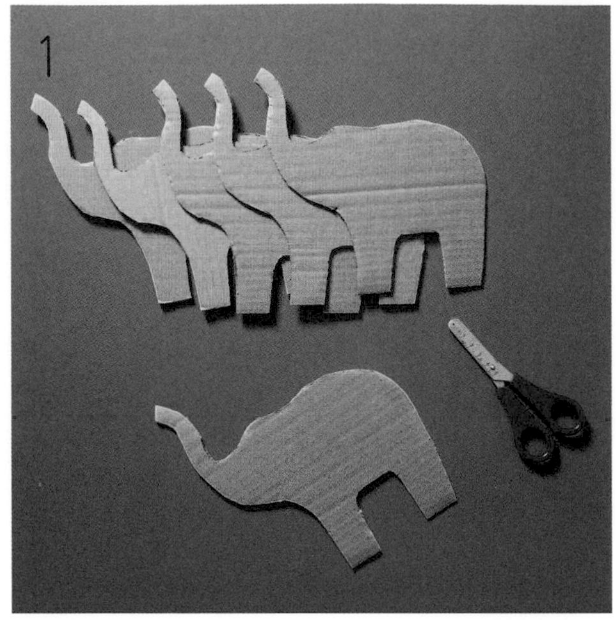

Draw an identical elephant shape (without ears) on cardboard six times. Ask for an adult's help to carefully cut out the elephants.

Cut the legs off two of the cardboard elephants, and cut the trunks off two different cardboard elephants.

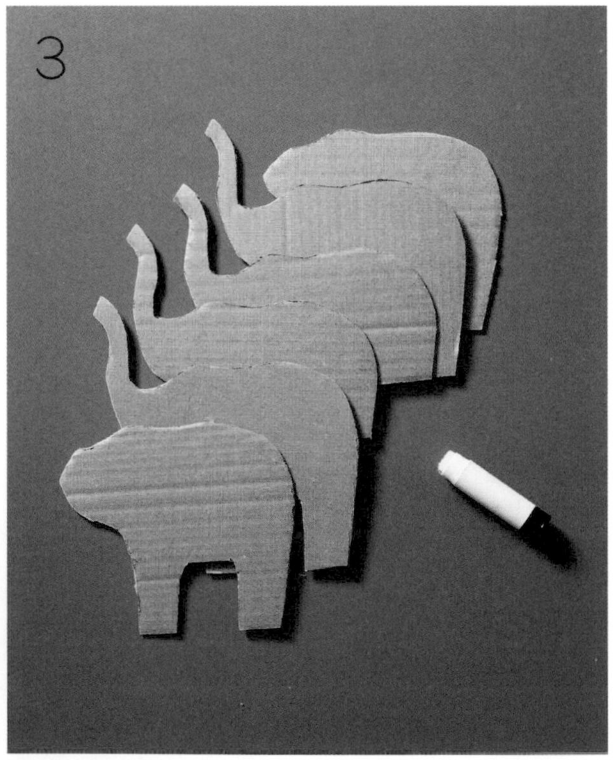

Next, stack the six cardboard shapes and glue them together. The order is: trunkless elephant, complete elephant, legless elephant, legless elephant, complete elephant, trunkless elephant.

Line up two pieces of different-colored yarn, and wrap them around the elephant's body once. Tie a knot to secure them, and then wrap the yarn around the body again and again.

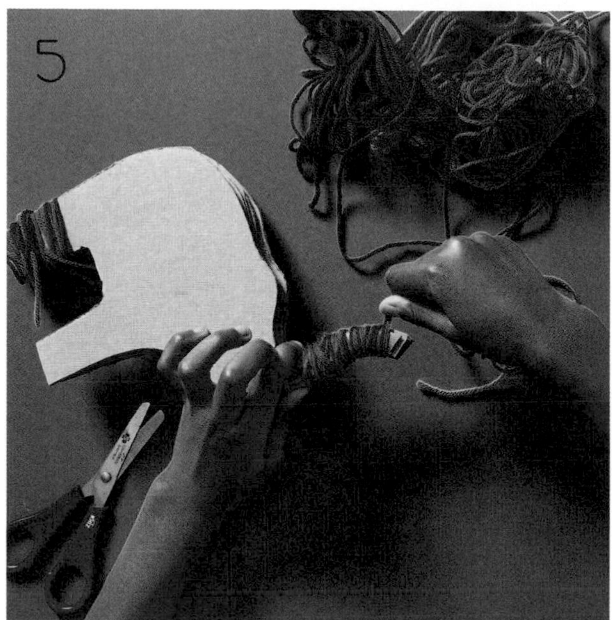

Keep wrapping your elephant in yarn until you can't see the cardboard anymore. Once you are finished, tie a double knot to secure the yarn on the sculpture.

Finally, cut two elephant ears from felt squares. Make the inside part of the ear extra long so that you can tuck the ears into the yarn that is already wrapped around the elephant's head!

Tip! Before wrapping the yarn around your elephant, check that your creature can stand. You might need to cut the feet to help it balance.

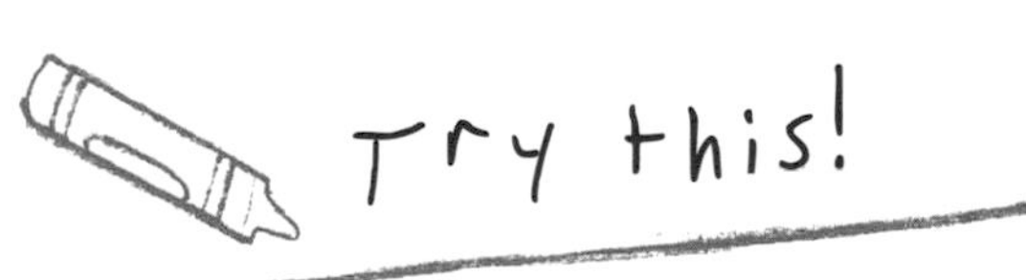

Why not turn the leftover yarn and a couple of popsicle sticks into a butterfly? First, glue the popsicle sticks into an X shape. Next, wind yarn around the center. Continue winding yarn around the two sticks on each side. Keep going until the wings are complete. Finally, bend a pipe cleaner in half around the center of the body. Thread beads over the pipe cleaner at both ends, and twist the pipe cleaner to secure them. Curl the pipe cleaner at the top to make antennae.

Silhouette stories

Kara Walker

Look at this!

Kara Walker, *Keys to the Coop*, 1997

African American artist Kara Walker is known for her paper cutouts and silhouette art. By turning complicated figures into simple outlines, she references eighteenth- and nineteenth-century silhouette art. She uses her art to challenge racial stereotypes.

Discuss this!

What story do you think this artwork shows? Who are the figures? The artwork shows a little girl and a chicken, but they might not be friends . . .

- Is the girl shouting? Can you see her tongue?
- What is the girl wearing? What is she holding?
- Where is the chicken's head?

Give it a try!

Now it's your turn to make paper cutout silhouettes to tell your own story.

You will need:

- 8.5x11 sheet of black paper
- 8.5x11 piece of cardboard
- Glue
- Pencil
- Scissors
- Tape
- Popsicle sticks
- Lamp (or strong sunlight)

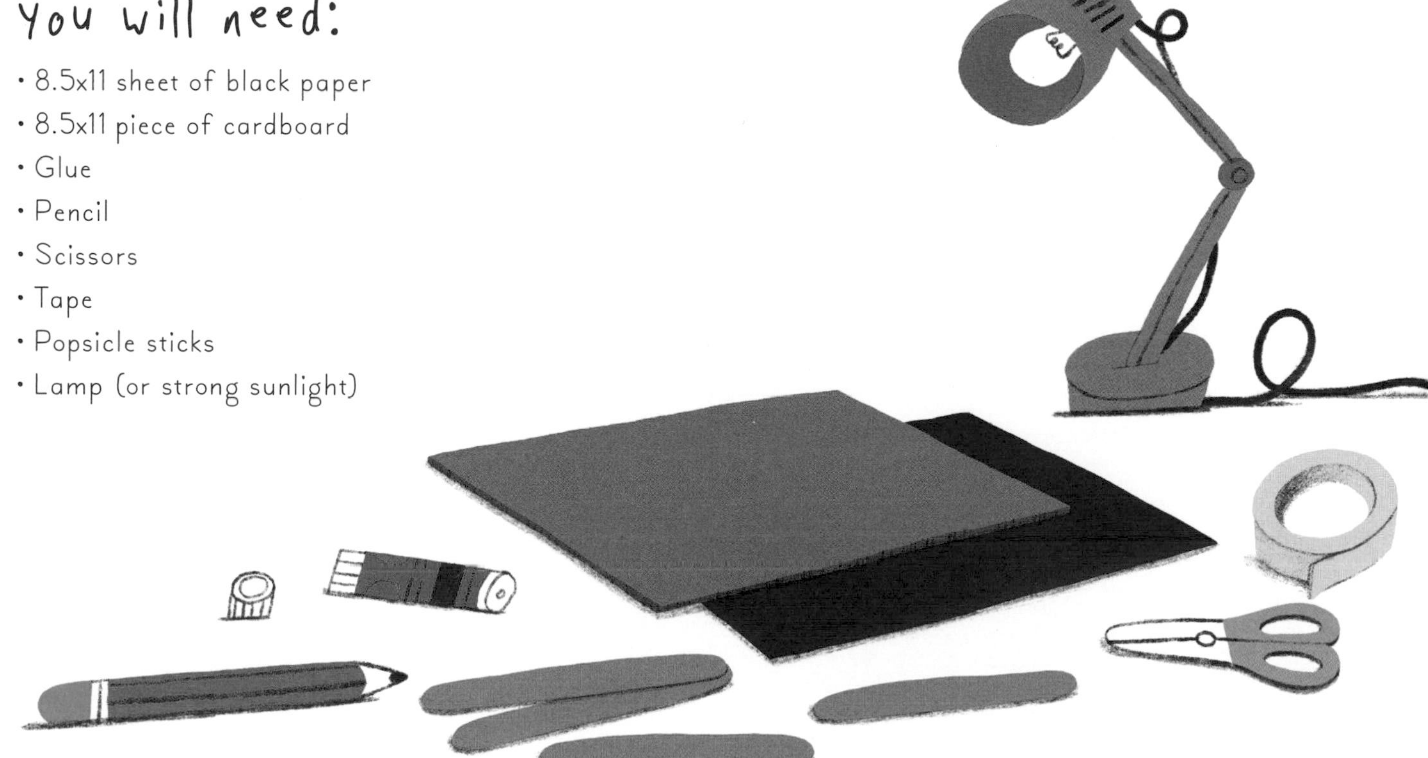

Take the sheet of black paper and glue it on top of the piece of cardboard.

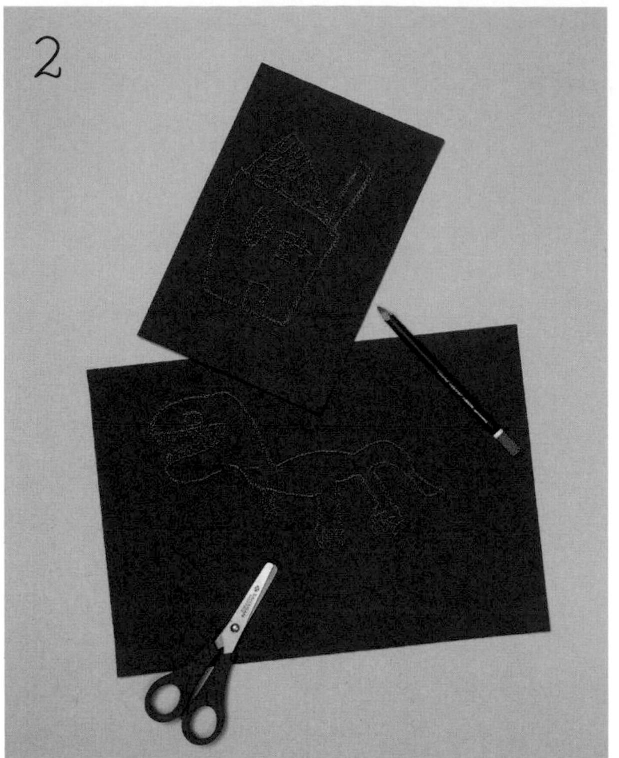

Decide what story you want to tell, and choose two characters. Use a pencil to draw the outlines of these two characters on the paper-covered cardboard.

Cut out the figures using scissors. (Mini artists should ask an adult for help.)

4

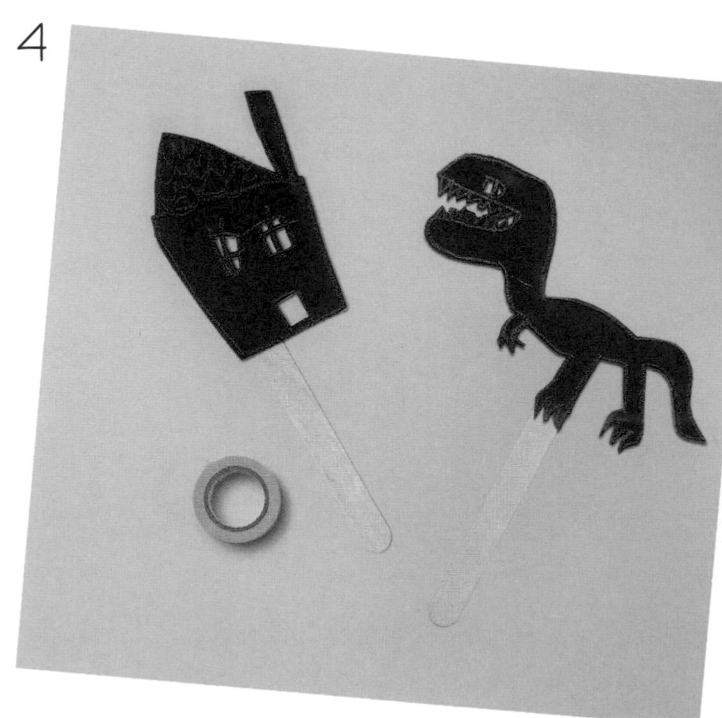

Use tape to stick each character onto a popsicle stick.

Turn on a lamp or go outside into strong sunlight. Hold the bottom of the popsicle sticks and position your characters between the source of light and a wall–their shadows will appear on the wall behind you.

Use these shadows to act out your story. You have just made your first shadow theater!

Tip! Draw your characters in profile (from the side) so that they are easy to identify. It helps to choose figures with a very recognizable shape.

Try this!

Find a photograph of yourself in profile. Using the photograph to help you, draw your own outline on a piece of black paper. Ask for an adult's help to cut out the outline, then glue it on a sheet of white paper. Now you can frame your own silhouette portrait!

Covered in dots

Yayoi Kusama

Look at this!

Yayoi Kusama, *The Obliteration Room*, 2002

Yayoi Kusama has been playing with dots for more than fifty years. Here, the artist covered a white room with colorful round stickers on every surface. She invited visitors to participate by adding stickers too. How fun is that?

Discuss this!

How does the color and chaos of this room make you feel?

- It looks like someone is having a party! Or maybe we've just arrived in Wonderland? Where do you think we are?
- Can you count the spots?
- How many colors can you see?
- Can you recognize any pieces of furniture?

Give it a try!

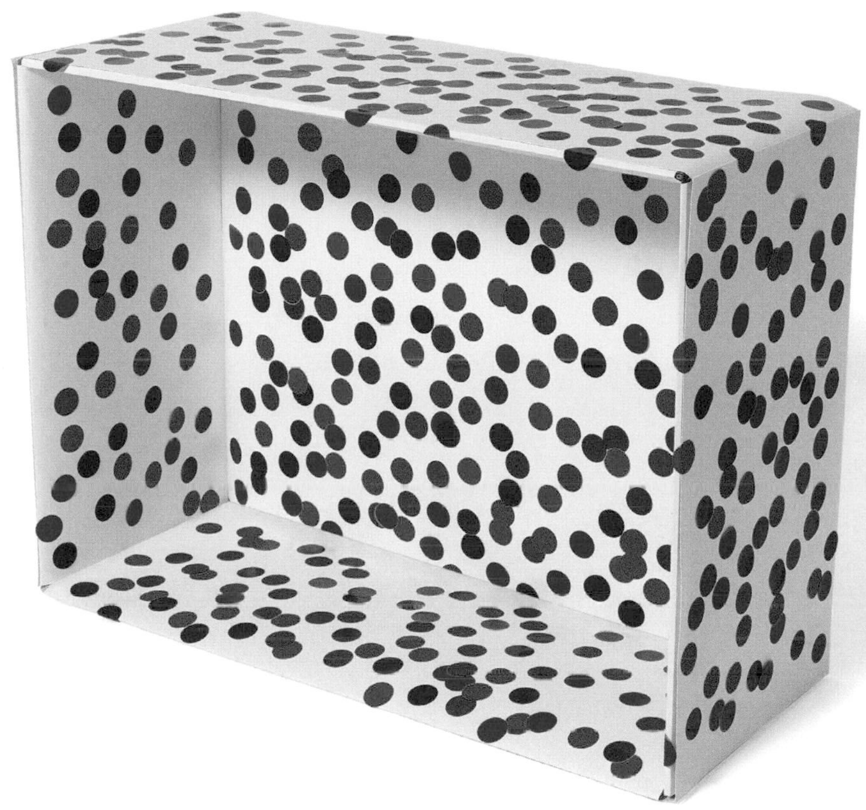

If you prefer your real-life walls and furniture to stay sticker-free, it's easy to build a miniature Obliteration Room. Give it plain white walls to begin with, then add as many stickers as you like!

You will need:

- Cardboard box
- Scissors
- Paper
- Glue or tape
- Lots of round, colorful stickers

1

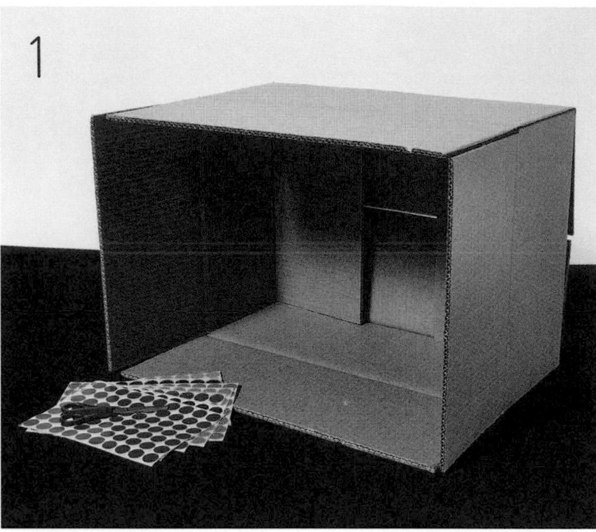

First, let's make the basic room. Place a cardboard box on its side so that you can see inside it.

2

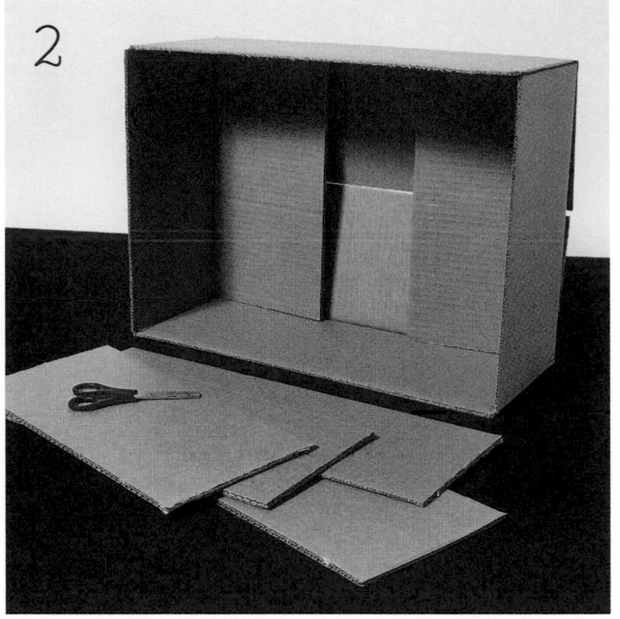

Cut off the flaps around the top edge of the box (you can save them for another *Mini Artists* project).

3

Glue or tape white paper all over the box, until it's covered inside and out.

4

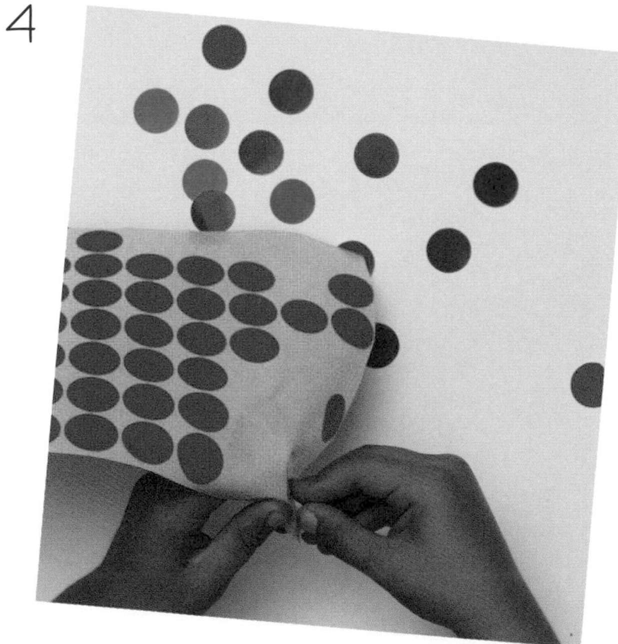

Now start covering the inside of your box-room with round stickers.

Tip! Try to cover the whole surface and leave as little empty space as you can. Don't be afraid to layer the stickers on top of each other.

5

Keep on sticking until the inside of the box is bursting with color. Try to mix up the colors as you work. Dots can overlap, too.

6

Finally, cover the outside of the box with dots. The brighter, the better! When you're finished, why not invite some toys to visit your *Obliteration Room*?

Yayoi Kusama loves pumpkins. Make your own by cutting four (or more) strips of paper. Lay them on top of each other, rotating them so that they form a star shape. Glue them together at the center. Lift the ends of each strip and stick them together at the top. You've made a 3D pumpkin! Add black stickers for a stem and dots.

List of Artworks

Page 7: Pablo Picasso, *Claude Drawing, Françoise and Paloma (Claude dessinant, Françoise et Paloma)*, 1954. Oil on canvas, 116 x 89 (45 ¾ x 35 ⅛). © Succession Picasso/DACS, London 2023. **Page 12:** *The dotted horse*, Pech Merle cave, France, c. 15000 BCE. Prisma Archivo/Alamy Stock Photo. **Page 16:** Account tablet of goats and sheep, Telloh (ancient Girsu), Sumer, c. 2350 BCE. Gianni Dagli Orti/Shutterstock **Page 20:** *Hippopotamus ("William")*, c. 1961-1878 BCE. From Middle Egypt, Meir, Tomb B3 of the monarch Senbi II, pit 1 (steward Senbi), Khashaba excavations, 1910, 20 x 7.5 x 11.2 (7 ⅞ x 3 x 4 ½). The Metropolitan Museum of Art, New York. Gift of Edward S. Harkness, 1917. **Page 24:** Fan Kuan, *Travelers by Streams and Mountains*, c. 1000. Hanging scroll, ink and light color on silk, 206.3 x 103.3 (81 ¼ x 40 ¾). Palace Museum, Taipei. **Page 28:** Stained glass windows inside the Sainte-Chapelle, Paris, France, 1242-48. Jan Willem van Hofwegen/Alamy Stock Photo. **Page 32:** Mask made of cedro wood and covered in turquoise mosaic with scattered turquoise cabochons, Aztec, c. 1400-1521. Photo © The Trustees of the British Museum. **Page 38:** Anni Albers, *Black White Red*, 1926/1964 (produced 1965). Silk and cotton, plain weave double cloth of paired warps and wefts, 179.4 x 122.2 (70 ⅝ x 48 ⅛). Originally produced by the Bauhaus Workshop (1919-1933), Dessau, Germany. Rewoven at Gunta Stölzl's Workshop, Zürich, Switzerland. The Art Institute of Chicago/Art Resource, NY/Scala, Florence. © The Josef and Anni Albers Foundation/Artists Rights Society (ARS), New York and DACS, London 2023. **Page 42:** Barbara Hepworth, *Oval Sculpture (No. 2)*, 1943, cast 1958. Plaster on wooden base, 29.3 x 40 x 25.5 (11 ⅝ x 15 ¾ x 10 ⅛). Photo Tate. Barbara Hepworth © Bowness. **Page 46:** Jackson Pollock, *Number 1, 1950 (Lavender Mist)*, 1950. Oil, enamel and aluminium on canvas, 221 x 299.7 (87 x 118). National Gallery of Art, Washington. Ailsa Mellon Bruce Fund. © The Pollock-Krasner Foundation ARS, NY and DACS, London 2023. **Page 50:** Wifredo Lam, *Untitled*, 1974. Silkscreen print in colors, 65 x 50 (25 ⅝ x 19 ¾). © Wifredo Lam Estate, Paris. © ADAGP, Paris and DACS, London 2023. **Page 54:** Henri Matisse, *The Sorrow of the King (La Tristesse du roi)*, 1952. Gouache paper, cut out, mounted on canvas, 292 x 386 (115 x 152). Photo Centre Pompidou, MNAM-CCI, Dist. RMN-Grand Palais/Philippe Migeat. © Succession H. Matisse/DACS 2023. **Page 58:** Louise Nevelson, *Total Totality II*, 1959-68. Painted wood, 258.1 x 429.9 x 24.8 (101 ⅝ x 169 ¼ x 9 ¾). Harvard Art Museums/Fogg Museum, Gift of Richard H. Solomon in honor of his parents, Mr. and Mrs. Sidney L. Solomon. Photo © President and Fellows of Harvard College. © ARS, NY and DACS, London 2023. **Page 62:** Hélio Oiticica, *Tropicália, Penetrables PN 2 "Purity is a myth" and PN 3 "Imagetical"*, 1966-67. Wooden structures, fabric, plastic, carpet, wire mesh, tulle, patchouli, sandalwood, television, sand, gravel, plants, birds and poems by Roberta Camila Salgado. Dimensions Variable. Courtesy Lisson Gallery. © César e Claudio Oiticica. **Page 68:** Jean-Michel Basquiat, *Trumpet*, 1984. Acrylic and oil stick painting on canvas, 152.4 x 152.4 (60 x 60). Licensed by Artestar, New York. © The Estate of Jean-Michel Basquiat/ADAGP, Paris and DACS, London 2023. **Page 72:** Tony Cragg, *New Figuration*, 1985. Plastic, 440 x 350 (173 ¼ x 137 ⅞). Photo Michael Richter. Tony Cragg © DACS 2023. **Page 76:** Christo and Jeanne-Claude, *The Floating Piers*, Lake Iseo, Italy, 2016. Photo Wolfgang Volz. © Christo and Jeanne-Claude Foundation © ADAGP, Paris and DACS, London 2023. **Page 80:** Andy Goldsworthy, *Rowan leaves laid around a hole*, Yorkshire Sculpture Park, 25 October, 1987. C-type, 76 x 74.5 (29.9 x 29.3). Courtesy Galerie Lelong & Co. © Andy Goldsworthy. **Page 84:** Mrinalini Mukherjee, *Aranyani*, 1996. Dyed Hemp, 142 x 127 x 104 (56 x 50 x 41). Photo Ravi Pasricha, Mrinalini Mukherjee Archive. Courtesy of the Mrinalini Mukherjee Foundation and Asia Art Archive. **Page 88:** Kara Walker, *Keys to the Coop*, 1997. Linocut, 101.6 x 153.7 (40 x 60.5). Courtesy Sikkema Jenkins & Co. and Sprüth Magers. © Kara Walker. **Page 92:** Yayoi Kusama, *The Obliteration Room*, 2002-present. Installation view in "Yayoi Kusama: Life is the Heart of a Rainbow", QAGOMA, Brisbane, 2017. Furniture, white paint, dot stickers, dimensions variable. Collaboration between Yayoi Kusama and Queensland Art Gallery. Commissioned Queensland Art Gallery. Gift of the artist through the Queensland Art Gallery Foundation 2012. Collection Queensland Art Gallery, Gallery of Modern Art. Photo Natasha Harth, QAGOMA. © YAYOI KUSAMA.

Photography by Lauren Winsor

First published in the United States of America in 2023 by Thames & Hudson Inc., 500 Fifth Avenue, New York, New York 10110

Library of Congress Control Number 2022952175

ISBN 978-0-500-66019-5

Printed and bound in China by C & C Offset Printing Co. Ltd

To L&V and all the artists out there (both great and mini) for constant inspiration. Thank you to Roger and Anna for championing *Mini Artists* at T&H and to Izzie, Kate, Lauren, Rachel, and Robert for turning an idea into a great book. - J.S.